BIDWELL'S GUIDE TO GOVERNMENT MINISTERS

VOLUME 2

The Arab World
1900–1972

Compiled and edited by

ROBIN BIDWELL

Secretary of the Middle East Centre, Cambridge

FRANK CASS & COMPANY LIMITED

First published 1973 in Great Britain by
FRANK CASS AND COMPANY LIMITED
67 Great Russell Street, London WC1B 3BT, England

and in United States of America by
FRANK CASS AND COMPANY LIMITED
c/o International Scholarly Book Services, Inc.
P.O. Box 4347, Portland, Oregon 97208

Copyright © 1973 Robin Bidwell

ISBN 0 7146 3001 2

Library of Congress Catalog Card No. 72-92958

All rights reserved. No part of this publication may be reproduced in any form or by any means, electronic, mechanical, photocopying, recording or otherwise, without the prior permission of Frank Cass and Company Limited in writing.

Printed in Great Britain by
Unwin Brothers Limited
The Gresham Press, Old Woking, Surrey, England
A member of the Staples Printing Group

To

BOB and MARION

with

Gratitude

and

Affection

How to use this book

I have divided the countries of the Arab World into four groups.

Group A comprises those countries where there was some form of Cabinet Government before 1945. These are
> Egypt (I have kept this name throughout for the sake of simplicity, even during the period when the country was known as the United Arab Republic)
> Syria
> Lebanon
> Iraq
> Jordan (Trans-Jordan before April 1949)

In addition to the usual Ministers, I have listed the British or French Representatives for the period before 1945.

Group B consists of those Arab countries which were under British or French rule or protection before achieving their complete independence. In this group will be found
> Morocco
> Algeria
> Tunisia
> Libya
> Sudan
> South Arabia (now The People's Democratic Republic of Yemen)

As with the previous group, I have added the names of Governors or Residents during the period before independence.

Group C consists of those Arab countries which, although never under Western rule, did not have formal Cabinets before 1945. They had, of course, Ministers, but these were the Representatives of the Ruler for a particular Department rather than members of a Cabinet as the term is generally understood. In this group will be found
> Saudi Arabia
> Yemen
> Kuwait
> Bahrain
> Qatar
> Oman, and the new
> Union of Arab Emirates

Group D contains the Trucial States. For these countries I have listed only the Rulers, for although some now have Cabinets, they are of too recent an origin to set out in the form of tables. I shall hope to do this in a subsequent edition.

Each Minister is listed with the date of his appointment and each new page begins with the names of those Ministers whose appointments were the last announced for those offices. Each Minister should be assumed to have continued in power until a new name appears in his column. Only his last name is given, and for further particulars it will be necessary to turn back to the date of his assumption of responsibility. An example will show how this works. If it is desired to find out who was the Iraqi Foreign Minister in June 1967, one must turn to the Foreign Ministers in Group A. One then takes the first date subsequent to June in the Iraqi column, which in this case is 10 July, and it will be seen that up to that date the post was held by Dr Adnan al-Pachachi.

R. B.

Contents

How to use this book	vii
Introduction	xi
HEADS OF STATE	
Group A	1
Group B	4
Group C	5
Group D	7
HEADS OF GOVERNMENT	
Group A	9
Group B	21
Group C	24
MINISTERS OF FOREIGN AFFAIRS	
Group A	27
Group B	39
Group C	42
MINISTERS OF WAR/DEFENCE	
Group A	45
Group B	57
Group C	60
MINISTERS OF THE INTERIOR	
Group A	63
Group B	77
Group C	80
MINISTERS OF FINANCE	
Group A	83
Group B	96
Group C	99
MINISTERS OF OIL	101
BRITISH/FRENCH REPRESENTATIVES	
Group A	103
BRITISH/FRENCH/ITALIAN REPRESENTATIVES	
Group B	105
BRITISH/FRENCH/ITALIAN FOREIGN AND COLONIAL MINISTERS	111
NOTES	121

Introduction

This Guide to Arab Ministers follows naturally upon my previous book which lists the Governments of Europe.* The Arab World is a natural unit and there is ever-increasing contact between the States which compose it: almost daily one reads in the Press of exchanges of official visits. I have therefore listed Ministers with the dates of their tenure of office so that it may be possible to see who was in power upon any particular day.

In order to avoid excessive bulk, I have restricted these tables to the Ministers of primary importance. I have listed the Heads of State, Premiers, and Ministers of Foreign Affairs, War, the Interior, Finance and Oil. In the same pursuit of clarity, I have kept notes to a minimum, so that this is in no sense a history of the Arab World. Where there has been an interregnum, I have not recorded the fact, but merely listed the new incumbents upon the day on which they entered office. Similarly, if a Minister has died in office I have not listed a short vacancy in the post. Where a new Minister is appointed *ad interim* I have indicated this with an asterisk if he did not subsequently keep the portfolio; but if he was subsequently confirmed in office, I have merely noted the first date. It has not always been possible to be entirely consistent in dates because some authorities may give the day upon which a Premier was appointed, while others may list that of his approval by Parliament or the final construction of his Cabinet, which may have spread over several days.

Similarly, I have made no attempt to be consistent over the transliteration of Arabic names. It is, of course, possible to adopt a regular system if one is dealing with places or with people long dead, but not with contemporaries who are, for the most part, highly literate in a European language. Many of the States publish official documents in a European language as well as in Arabic. While Tunisian State papers name the President as Habib Bourguiba, it would be absurd for me to insist upon calling him al-Habīb abu Raqībah and would serve only to confuse people dependent entirely upon Western sources. I very much hope that an Arabic version of this book will appear in due course so that the Arabist may see the names in their original form.

A note on sources may be of use to readers who require fuller details of Cabinets than are given in this work. For the period before 1918 when only Egypt had Ministers, full particulars may be found in *The Times* and its index. From 1921 until about 1940, the best source is *Oriente Moderno*. This journal is not fully comprehensive and needs to be checked against the diplomatic records in the Public Record Office, which are open up to 1945. From 1947, the *Middle East Journal* is useful but sometimes omits changes within Cabinets. From 1951, the BBC Monitoring Service *Summary of World Broadcasts* contains much of but not all the information required. Since its appearance in 1966 *The Arab Report and Record* is the most valuable source.

While, naturally, all mistakes are my own, I should like to record my thanks for help on specific points to H.E. the Yemeni Ambassador and Mr Hamad al-Saidan of the Kuwaiti Embassy.

Cambridge, January 1973   ROBIN BIDWELL

Bidwell's Guide to Government Ministers, Volume 1: *The Major Powers and Western Europe, 1900-1971* (Frank Cass, London, 1973)

HEADS OF STATE

HS (A)

		EGYPT	SYRIA	LEBANON	IRAQ	TRANS-JORDAN
1900	1 Jan	Abbas II Hilmi				
1914	19 Dec	Husayn Kamil				
1917	9 Oct	Ahmad Fuad				
1920	8 Mar		Faysal			
	25 July		*None (Note 1)*			
1921	Apr					Abdallah
	23 Aug				Faysal	
1925	1 Jan		Subhi Barakat			
	21 Dec		*None (Note 2)*			
1926	26 May			Charles Dabbas		
1932	11 June		Muhammad Ali al-Abid			
1933	8 Sept				Ghazi	
1934	31 Jan			Habib Pasha al-Sa'd		
1936	20 Jan			Emile Eddé		
	28 Apr	Faruq				
	21 Dec		Hashim al-Atasi			
1939	4 Apr				Faysal II	
1941	4 Apr		Khalid Pasha al-Azm			
	27 Sept		Shaykh Taj al-Din al-Hasani			
	1 Dec			Alfred Naqqash		
1943	22 Mar			Ayyub Thabit *(Note 3)*		
	25 Mar		Ata Bey al-Ayyubi *(Note 3)*			
	21 July			Petro Trad		
	17 Aug		Shukri al-Quwatli			
	21 Sept			Bishara al-Khuri		
1949	30 Mar		*None*			
	25 June		General Husni al-Zaim			
	19 Dec		Hashim al-Atasi			

1

HS (A)

	EGYPT	SYRIA	LEBANON	IRAQ	JORDAN
	Faruq	al-Atasi	al-Khuri	Faysal II	Abdallah
1951 20 July					Talal
3 Dec		Colonel Fawzi Silo			
1952 26 July	Ahmad Fuad II				
11 Aug					Husayn
24 Sept			Camille Chamoun		
1953 18 June	General Muhammad Neguib				
10 July		Brigadier Adib al-Shishakli			
1954 1 Mar		Hashim al-Atasi			
14 Nov	None				
1955 18 Aug		Shukri al-Quwatli			
1956 24 June	Colonel Gemal Abd al-Nasir				
1958 5 Feb		Colonel Gemal Abd al-Nasir *(Note 4)*			
14 July				None *(Note 5)*	
31 July			General Fuad Shihab		
1961 30 Sept		*None* *(Note 6)*			
14 Dec		Nazim al-Qudsi			
1963 8 Feb				Field Marshal Abd al-Salam Muhammad Arif	
9 Mar		General Luay al-Atasi *(Note 7)*			
27 July		General Amin al-Hafiz			
1964 18 Aug			Charles Hilu		
1966 23 Feb		Nur al-Din al-Atasi			
16 Apr				General Abd al-Rahman Muhammad Arif	

2

	EGYPT	SYRIA	LEBANON	IRAQ	JORDAN
	Abd al-Nasir	al-Atasi	Hilu	Arif	Husayn
1968 18 July				General Ahmad Hassan al-Bakr	
1970 17 Aug			Sulayman Franjiyeh		
17 Oct	Anwar Sadat				
19 Nov		Ahmad al-Khatib			
1971 22 Feb		General Hafiz al-Asad			

HS (B) **HEADS OF STATE**

	MOROCCO	ALGERIA	TUNISIA	LIBYA	SUDAN	SOUTHERN YEMEN
1900 1 Jan	Mulai Abd al-Aziz ben Hassan		Ali ben Ahsin Bey			
1902 11 June			Muhammad al-Hadi Bey			
1906 12 May			Muhammad al-Nasr Bey			
1908 4 Jan	Mulai Hafid ben Hassan (Note 8)					
1912 18 Aug	Mulai Yussef ben Hassan					
1922 8 July			Muhammad al-Habib Bey			
1927 Nov	Sidi Muhammad ben Yussef					
1929 11 Feb			Ahmad Bey			
1942 19 June			Muhammad al-Munsif Bey			
1943 15 May			Muhammad al-Amin Bey			
1951 24 Dec				Idris		
1953 20 Aug	*(Sidi Muhammad ben Arafa) (Note 9)*					
1957 25 July			Habib Bourguiba			
1958 17 Nov					General Ibrahim Abboud (Note 10)	
1961 27 Feb	Hassan II					
1962 25 Sept		Ferhat Abbas				
1963 15 Sept		Ahmad ben Bella				
1964 15 Nov					*None*	
1965 19 June		*None*				
8 July					Ismail al-Azhari	
1967 30 Nov						Qahtan al-Shaabi
1969 25 May					General Jaafer al-Nimeiri (Note 11)	
24 June						Salem Robai
1 Sept				*None*		

4

HEADS OF STATE

HS (C)

	SAUDI ARABIA	YEMEN	KUWAIT	BAHRAIN	QATAR	OMAN	UNION OF ARAB EMIRATES
1900 1 Jan		Muhammad ben Yahya	Mubarak al-Sabah	Isa ben Ali (Note 12)	Jasim ben Muhammad (Note 13)	Faysal ben Turki	
1902 Jan	Abd al-Aziz ibn Abd al-Rahman ibn Saud (Note 14)						
1904		Yahya ben Muhammad					
1913					Abdallah ben Jasim		
5 Oct						Taimur ben Faysal	
1915 Nov			Jabir ben Mubarak				
1917 5 Feb			Salim ben Mubarak				
1921 23 Feb			Ahmad al-Jabir				
1932 10 Feb						Said ben Taimur	
9 Dec				Hamad ben Isa			
1942 3 Feb				Salman ben Hamad			
1948 Feb		Ahmad ben Yahya					
1949 20 Aug					Ali ben Abdallah		
1950 30 Jan			Abdallah al-Salim				
1953 9 Nov	Saud ben Abd al-Aziz						
1960 24 Oct					Ahmad ben Ali		
1961 2 Nov				Isa ben Salman			
1962 19 Sept		Muhammad al-Badr ben Ahmad					
28 Sept		*None*					
31 Oct		Field Marshal Abdallah al-Sallal					
1964 2 Nov	Faysal ben Abd al-Aziz						
1965 24 Nov			Sabah al-Salim				
1967 5 Nov		Qadi Abd al-Rahman al-Iryani					

HS (C)

	SAUDI ARABIA	YEMEN	KUWAIT	BAHRAIN	QATAR	OMAN	UNION OF ARAB EMIRATES
	Faysal	al-Iryani	Sabah al-Salim	Isa	Ahmad	Said	
1970 23 July						Qabus ben Said	
1971 9 Dec							Zaid ben Sultan al-Nayahan
1972 22 Feb					Khalifa ben Hamad		

HEADS OF STATE

HS (D)

		ABU DHABI	DUBAI	SHARJAH	FUJAYRAH	UMM AL-QAWAIN	AJMAN	RAS AL-KHAYMAH
1900	1 Jan	Zaid ben Khalifa al-Nahayan	Maktum ben Hashar al-Maktum	Saqr ben Khalid al-Qasimi	*Note 15*	Ahmad ben Abdallah al-Mualla	Humaid ben Rashid al-Na'imi	Humaid ben Abdallah al-Qasimi
	8 July						Abd al-Aziz ben Humaid	
	Sept							<u>Incorporated in Sharjah</u>
1904	13 June					Rashid ben Ahmad		
1906	16 Feb		Buti ben Suhail					
1909	May	Tahnun ben Zaid						
1910	Feb						Humaid ben Abd al-Aziz	
1912	Oct	Hamdan ben Zaid						
	Nov		Said ben Maktum					
1914	Apr			Khalid ben Ahmad				
1921	Oct							Sultan ben Salim
1922	Aug	Sultan ben Zaid				Abdallah ben Rashid		
1923	Oct					Hamad ben Ibrahim		
1924				Sultan ben Saqr				
1926	4 Aug	Saqr ben Zaid						
1928	Apr	Shakhbut ben Sultan						
	Jan						Rashid ben Humaid	
1929	Feb					Ahmad ben Rashid		
1948	Feb							Saqr ben Muhammad
1951	May			Saqr ben Sultan				
1952	Mar				Muhammad ben Hamad al-Sharqi *(Note 16)*			
1958	Oct		Rashid ben Said *(Note 17)*					
1965	25 June			Khalid ben Muhammad				
1966	2 Aug	Zaid ben Sultan						
1972	25 Jan			Sultan ben Muhammad				

.7

HEADS OF GOVERNMENT

HG (A)

		EGYPT	SYRIA	LEBANON	IRAQ	TRANS-JORDAN
1900	1 Jan	Mustafa Fahmy Pasha				
1908	12 Nov	Boutros Ghali Pasha				
1910	22 Feb	Muhammad Said Pasha				
1914	5 Apr	Husayn Rushdi Pasha				
1919	Mar	*None*				
	9 Apr	Husayn Rushdi Pasha				
	12 Apr	*None*				
	21 May	Muhammad Said Pasha				
	19 Nov	Yusuf Wahba Pasha				
1920	8 Mar		Ali Ridha al-Rikabi *(Note 18)*			
	3 May		Hashim al-Atasi			
	20 May	Muhammad Tawfiq Nasim Pasha				
	25 July		*None (Note 1)*			
	11 Nov				The Naqib of Baghdad Saiyyid Abd al-Rahman al-Gaylani *(Note 19)*	
1921	16 Mar	Adli Yeghen Pasha				
1922	1 Mar	Abd al-Khalek Sarwat Pasha				
	20 Nov				Abd al-Muhsin al-Sa'dun	
	30 Nov	Muhammad Tawfiq Nasim Pasha				
1923	6 Feb					Muzhir Bey Raslan
	15 Mar	Yahya Ibrahim Pasha				

HG (A)

		EGYPT	SYRIA	LEBANON	IRAQ	TRANS-JORDAN
		Ibrahim Pasha	*None*		al-Sa'dun	Raslan
1923	June		Subhi Bey Barakat *(Note 20)*			
	5 Sept					Hassan Khalid Pasha Abu al-Huda
	22 Nov				General Ja'far Pasha al-Askari	
1924	26 Jan	Sa'd Zaghlul Pasha				
	3 May					Ali Ridha al-Rikabi
	2 Aug				Yasin al-Hashimi	
	24 Nov	Ahmad Ziwer Pasha				
1925	26 June				Abd al-Muhsin al-Sa'dun	
	21 Dec		*None (Note 2)*			
1926	28 Apr		Damad Ahmad Nami			
	31 May			Auguste Adib Pasha		
	7 June	Adli Yeghen Pasha				
	24 July					Hassan Khalid Pasha Abu al-Huda
	21 Nov				General Ja'far Pasha al-Askari	
1927	26 Apr	Abd al-Khalek Sarwat Pasha				
	5 May			Bishara Bey al-Khuri		
1928	11 Jan				Abd al-Muhsin al-Sa'dun	
	15 Feb		Shaykh Taj al-Din al-Hasani			
	16 Mar	Mustafa Nahas Pasha				

HG (A)

		EGYPT	SYRIA	LEBANON	IRAQ	TRANS-JORDAN
		Nahas	al-Hasani	al-Khuri	al-Sa'dun	Abu al-Huda
1928	27 June	Muhammad Mahmud Pasha				
	10 Aug			Habib Pasha al-Sa'd		
1929	28 Apr				Tawfiq Bey al-Suwaydi	
	9 May			Bishara Bey al-Khuri		
	19 Sept				Abd al-Muhsin al-Sa'dun	
	4 Oct	Adli Yeghen Pasha				
	11 Oct			Emile Eddé		
	18 Nov				Naji al-Suwaydi	
1930	1 Jan	Mustafa Nahas Pasha				
	23 Mar				General Nuri Pasha al-Said	
	25 Mar			Auguste Adib Pasha		
	20 June	Ismail Sidqi Pasha				
1931	21 Feb					Abdallah al-Sarraj
	Nov		*None (Note 2)*			
1932	May			*None (Note 2)*		
	7 June		Haqqi al-Azm Pasha			
	3 Nov				Naji Shawkat	
1933	20 Mar				Rashid Ali al-Gaylani	
	21 Sept	Abd al-Fattah Yahia Pasha				
	9 Nov				Jamil al-Midfa'i	
	18 Nov					Ibrahim Bey Hashim

11

HG (A)

	EGYPT	SYRIA	LEBANON	IRAQ	TRANS-JORDAN
	Yahia	al-Azm	None	al-Midfa'i	Hashim
1934 16 Mar		Shaykh Taj al-Din al-Hasani			
27 Aug				Ali Jawdat	
15 Nov	Muhammad Tawfiq Nasim Pasha				
1935 4 Mar				Jamil al-Midfa'i	
17 Mar				Yasin Pasha al-Hashimi	
1936 30 Jan	Ali Mahir Pasha				
22 Feb		Ata Bey al-Ayyubi			
9 May	Mustafa Nahas Pasha				
30 Oct				Hikmat Sulayman	
21 Dec		Jamil Bey Mardam			
1937 5 Jan			Khair al-Din al-Ahdab		
17 Aug				Jamil al-Midfa'i	
29 Dec	Muhammad Mahmud Pasha				
1938 18 Mar			Amir Khalid Shihab		
28 Sept					Tawfiq Pasha Abu al-Huda
24 Oct			Abdallah al-Yafi		
25 Dec				General Nuri Pasha al-Said	
1939 23 Feb		Lutfi al-Haffar			
6 Apr		Nasuhi al-Bukhari			
10 July		Bahij al-Khatib *(Note 21)*			
18 Aug	Ali Mahir Pasha				

HG (A)

	EGYPT	SYRIA	LEBANON	IRAQ	TRANS-JORDAN
	Mahir	al-Khatib	al-Yafi	al-Said	Abu al-Huda
1939 21 Sept			*None (Note 22)*		
1940 31 Mar				Rashid Ali al-Gaylani	
28 June	Hassan Sabri Pasha				
15 Nov	Husayn Sirri Pasha				
1941 3 Feb				General Taha Pasha al-Hashimi	
4 Apr		Khalid Pasha al-Azm			
7 Apr			Alfred Naqqash		
13 Apr				Rashid Ali al-Gaylani	
2 June				Jamil al-Midfa'i	
21 Sept		Hassan al-Hakim			
10 Oct				General Nuri Pasha al-Said	
1 Dec			Ahmad al-Da'uq		
1942 6 Feb	Mustafa Nahas Pasha				
19 Apr		Husni al-Barazi			
July			Samih al-Sulh		
1943 10 Jan		Jamil al-Ulshi			
22 Mar			Ayyub Thabit *(Note 3)*		
25 Mar		Ata Bey al-Ayyubi *(Note 3)*			
1 Aug			Petro Trad		
19 Aug		Sa'd Allah al-Jabiri			
25 Sept			Riad al-Sulh		
1944 4 June				Hamdi al-Pachachi	

HG (A)

	EGYPT	SYRIA	LEBANON	IRAQ	TRANS-JORDAN
	Nahas	al-Jabiri	al-Sulh	al-Pachachi	Abu al-Huda
1944 9 Oct	Ahmad Mahir Pasha				
14 Oct		Faris al-Khuri			
1945 10 Jan			Abd al-Hamid Karami		
25 Feb	Mahmud Fahmy al-Nuqrashi Pasha				
19 May					Ibrahim Hashim Bey
23 Aug			Samih al-Sulh		
1 Oct		Sa'd Allah al-Jabiri			
1946 17 Feb	Ismail Sidqi Pasha				
23 Feb				Tawfiq al-Suwaydi	
22 May			Saadi al-Munlah		
1 June				Arshad al-Umari	
21 Nov				General Nuri Pasha al-Said	
10 Dec	Mahmud Fahmy al-Nuqrashi Pasha				
15 Dec			Riad al-Sulh		
28 Dec		Jamil Bey Mardam			
1947 6 Feb					Samir Pasha al-Rifai
29 Mar				Salih Jabir	
31 Dec					Tawfiq Pasha Abu al-Huda
1948 29 Jan				Muhammad al-Sadr	
26 June				Muzahim al-Pachachi	
16 Dec		Khalid Pasha al-Azm			

14

	EGYPT	SYRIA	LEBANON	IRAQ	JORDAN
	al-Nuqrashi	al-Azm	al-Sulh	al-Pachachi	Abu al-Huda
1948 28 Dec	Ibrahim Abd al-Hadi Pasha				
1949 6 Jan				General Nuri Pasha al-Said	
17 Apr		General Husni al-Zaim			
26 June		Muhsin al-Barazi			
26 July	Husayn Sirri Pasha				
17 Aug		Hashim al-Atasi			
10 Dec				Ali Jawdat	
24 Dec		Nazim al-Qudsi *(Note 23)*			
27 Dec		Khalid Pasha al-Azm			
1950 12 Jan	Mustafa Nahas Pasha				
5 Feb				Tawfiq al-Suwaydi	
13 Apr					Said al-Mufti
4 June		Nazim al-Qudsi			
15 Sept				General Nuri Pasha al-Said	
4 Dec					Samir Pasha al-Rifai
1951 13 Feb			Husayn al-Uwayni		
27 Mar		Khalid Pasha al-Azm			
7 June			Abdallah al-Yafi		
25 July					Tawfiq Pasha Abu al-Huda
9 Aug		Hassan al-Hakim			
28 Nov		Dr Ma'ruf al-Dawalibi			

HG (A)

	EGYPT	SYRIA	LEBANON	IRAQ	JORDAN
	Nahas	al-Dawalibi	al-Yafi	al-Said	Abu al-Huda
1951 3 Dec		Colonel Fawzi Silo			
1952 27 Jan	Ali Mahir Pasha				
11 Feb			Samih al-Sulh		
2 Mar	Nagib al-Hilali Pasha				
2 July	Husayn Sirri Pasha				
12 July				Mustafa al-Umari	
22 July	Nagib al-Hilali Pasha				
23 July	Ali Mahir Pasha				
7 Sept	General Muhammad Neguib				
10 Sept			Nazim Akkari		
18 Sept			General Fuad Shihab		
24 Sept			Abdallah al-Yafi *(Note 24)*		
1 Oct			Amir Khalid Shihab		
23 Nov				General Nur al-Din Mahmud	
1953 29 Jan				Jamil al-Midfa'i	
1 May			Saeb Salem		
5 May					Fawzi al-Mulqi
19 July		President Brigadier Adib al-Shishakli			
13 Aug			Abdallah al-Yafi		
17 Sept				Muhammad Fadil Jamali	
1954 25 Feb	Colonel Gemal Abd al-Nasir				

	EGYPT	SYRIA	LEBANON	IRAQ	JORDAN
	Abd al-Nasir	al-Shishakli	al-Yafi	Jamali	al-Mulqi
1954 1 Mar		Sabri al-Asali			
8 Mar	General Muhammad Neguib				
18 Apr	Colonel Gemal Abd al-Nasir				
29 Apr				Arshad al-Umari	
4 May					Tawfiq Abu al-Huda
18 June		Said al-Ghazzi			
4 Aug				General Nuri Pasha al-Said	
17 Sept			Samih al-Sulh		
3 Nov		Faris al-Khuri			
1955 13 Feb		Sabri al-Asali			
30 May					Said al-Mufti
13 Sept		Said al-Ghazzi			
19 Sept			Rashid Karami		
15 Dec					Haza' al-Majali
20 Dec					Ibrahim Hashim
1956 9 Jan					Samir al-Rifai
20 Mar			Abdallah al-Yafi		
22 May					Said al-Mufti
14 June		Sabri al-Asali			
1 July					Ibrahim Hashim
29 Oct					Sulayman al-Nabulsi
27 Nov			Samih al-Sulh		
1957 13 Apr					Abd al-Halim al-Nimr *(Note 25)*
15 Apr					Husayn Fakhri al-Khalidi
25 Apr					Ibrahim Hashim

HG (A)

	EGYPT	SYRIA	LEBANON	IRAQ	JORDAN
	Abd al-Nasir	al-Asali	al-Sulh	al-Said	Hashim
1957 20 June				Ali Jawdat	
15 Dec				Abd al-Wahhab Murjan	
1958 3 Mar				General Nuri Pasha al-Said	
6 Mar		*None (Note 26)*			
18 May				Ahmad Mukhtar Baban	Samir al-Rifai *(Note 27)*
14 July				General Abd al-Karim Qasim	
24 Sept			Rashid Karami		
1959 6 May					Haza' al-Majali
1960 14 May			Ahmad al-Da'uq		
2 Aug			Saeb Salem		
29 Aug					Bahjat al-Talhouni
1961 30 Sept		Dr Ma'mun Kuzbari			
31 Oct			Rashid Karami		
20 Nov		Izzat al-Nus			
22 Dec		Ma'ruf al-Dawalibi			
1962 27 Jan					Wasfi al-Tall
16 Apr		Dr Bashir al-Azmah			
17 Sept		Khalid Pasha al-Azm			
29 Sept	Ali Sabri *(Note 28)*				
1963 8 Feb				General Ahmad Hassan al-Bakr	
9 Mar		Salah al-Din Bitar			
27 Mar					Samir al-Rifai
21 Apr					Sharif Husayn ben Nasr

18

HG (A)

	EGYPT	SYRIA	LEBANON	IRAQ	JORDAN
	Sabri	Bitar	Karami	al-Bakr	ben Nasr
1963 12 Nov		General Amin al-Hafiz			
20 Nov				General Tahir Yahya	
1964 20 Feb			Husayn al-Uwayni		
13 May		Salah al-Din Bitar			
7 July					Bahjat al-Talhouni
4 Oct		General Amin al-Hafiz			
1965 13 Feb					Wasfi al-Tall
25 July			Rashid Karami		
6 Sept				Arif Abd al-Razzaq	
21 Sept				Abd al-Rahman al-Bazzaz	
23 Sept		Yusuf Zu'ayyin			
30 Sept	Zakariah Mohieddin				
1966 1 Jan		Salah al-Din Bitar			
25 Feb		Yusuf Zu'ayyin			
9 Apr			Abdallah al-Yafi		
9 Aug				General Naji Talib	
10 Sept	Muhammad Sidqi Sulayman				
7 Dec			Rashid Karami		
1967 4 Mar					Sharif Husayn ben Nasr
23 Apr					Saad Jumaa
10 May				President General Abd al-Rahman Muhammad Arif	
19 June	President Colonel Gemal Abd al-Nasir				

HG (A)

	EGYPT	SYRIA	LEBANON	IRAQ	JORDAN
	Abd al-Nasir	Zu'ayyin	Karami	Arif	Jumaa
1967 10 July				General Tahir Yahya	
7 Oct					Bahjat al-Talhouni
1968 8 Feb			Abdallah al-Yafi		
17 July				Colonel Abd al-Razzaq al-Nayif	
31 July				General Ahmad Hassan al-Bakr	
29 Oct		President Dr Nur al-Din al-Atasi			
1969 15 Jan			Rashid Karami		
24 Mar					Abd al-Moneim Rifai
12 Aug					Bahjat al-Talhouni
1970 26 June					Abd al-Moneim Rifai
16 Sept					Brigadier Muhammad Daoud
26 Sept					Ahmad Tuqan
13 Oct			Saeb Salem		
21 Oct	Dr Mahmud Fawzi				
28 Oct					Wasfi al-Tall
21 Nov		General Hafiz al-Asad			
1971 3 Apr		General Abd al-Rahman Khulaifawi			
29 Nov					Ahmad Lawzi
1972 17 Jan	Dr Aziz Sidqi				
21 Dec		Mahmud al-Ayyubi			

HEADS OF GOVERNMENT

HG (B)

	MOROCCO	ALGERIA	TUNISIA	LIBYA	SUDAN	SOUTHERN YEMEN
1947 29 July			Mustafa Kaak *(Note 29)*			
1950 17 Aug			Muhammad Chenik			
1951 29 Mar				Mahmud Muntasir		
1952 12 Apr			Salah al-Din Baccouche			
1954 6 Jan					Ismail al-Azhari	
18 Feb				Muhammad al-Saghisli		
2 Mar			Muammad Salah M'zali			
12 Apr				Mustafa ben Halim		
7 Aug			Tahar ben Ammar			
1955 7 Dec	M'barek Bekkai					
1956 14 Apr			Habib Bourguiba			
7 July					Abdallah Khalil	
1957 26 May				Abd al-Majid Qubar		
25 July			*None*			
1958 8 May	Ahmad Balafrej					
19 Sept		Ferhat Abbas *(Note 30)*				
18 Nov					General Ibrahim Abboud	
24 Dec	Abdallah Ibrahim					
1960 26 May	King Muhammad V					
17 Oct				Muhammad ben Othman		
1961 27 Feb	King Hassan II					
27 Aug		Yusuf ben Khedda *(Note 30)*				
1962 28 Sept		Ahmad ben Bella				
1963 19 Mar				Muhi al-Din Fikini		
13 Nov	Ahmad Bahnini					

HG (B)

	MOROCCO	ALGERIA	TUNISIA	LIBYA	SUDAN	SOUTHERN YEMEN
	Bahnini	ben Bella	*None*	Fikini	Abboud	
1964 22 Jan				Mahmud Muntasir		
30 Oct					Sirr al-Khatim al-Khalifa	
1965 18 Mar				Husayn Mazik		
8 June	King Hassan II					
10 June					Muhammad Ahmad Mahgoub	
19 June		*None*				
10 July		Colonel Houari Boumedienne				
1966 27 July					Saadiq al-Mahdi	
1967 18 May					Muhammad Ahmad Mahgoub	
2 July				Abd al-Qadir Badri		
6 July	Muhammad Benhima					
25 Oct				Abd al-Hamid Bakkush		
1 Dec						Qahtan al-Shaabi
1968 4 Sept				Wanis al-Qaddafi		
1969 6 Apr						Faysal Abd al-Latif
25 May					Babikr Awadhallah	
23 June						Muhammad Ali Haitham
8 Sept				Mahmud al-Maghrabi		
7 Oct	Ahmad Laraki					
28 Oct					General Jaafar al-Nimeiri	
7 Nov			Bahi Ladgham			
1970 16 Jan				Colonel Muammar al-Qaddafi		
2 Nov			Hedi Nouira			
1971 6 Aug	Karim Lamrani					

	MOROCCO	ALGERIA	TUNISIA	LIBYA	SUDAN	SOUTHERN YEMEN
	Lamrani	Houari Boumedienne	Hedi Nouira	Muammar al-Qaddafi	Jaafar al-Nimeiri	Haitham
1971 2 Aug						Ali Nasir Muhammad Hassani
1972 10 July				Major Abd al-Salam Jaloud		
3 Nov	Ahmad Uthman					

HEADS OF GOVERNMENT

	SAUDI ARABIA	YEMEN	KUWAIT	BAHRAIN	QATAR	OMAN	UNION OF ARAB EMIRATES
1953 9 Oct	Crown Prince Saud ben Abd al-Aziz *(Note 31)*						
1954 16 Aug	Crown Prince Faysal ben Abd al-Aziz						
1955 31 Aug		Imam Ahmad ben Yahya *(Note 32)*					
1960 21 Dec	King Saud ben Abd al-Aziz						
1962 19 Sept		Imam Muhammad al-Badr ben Ahmad					
28 Sept		General Abdallah al-Sallal					
16 Oct			Shaykh Sabah al-Salim al-Sabah				
31 Oct	Crown Prince Faysal ben Abd al-Aziz						
1963 25 Apr		Abd al-Latif Dayfallah					
5 Oct		Qadi Abd al-Rahman al-Iryani					
1964 10 Feb		General Hassan al-Amri					
29 Apr		General Hammud al-Jayifi					
1965 6 Jan		General Hassan al-Amri					
20 Apr		Ahmad Muhammad Noman					
11 July		President Abdallah al-Sallal					
20 July		General Hassan al-Amri					
30 Nov			Shaykh Jabir al-Ahmad				
1966 18 Sept		President Abdallah al-Sallal					

HG (C)

	SAUDI ARABIA	YEMEN	KUWAIT	BAHRAIN	QATAR	OMAN	UNION OF ARAB EMIRATES
	Faysal	al-Sallal	al-Ahmad				
1967 5 Nov		Muhsin al-Aini					
21 Dec		General Hassan al-Amri					
1969 9 July		*Abd al-Salam Sabra					
2 Sept		Abdallah al-Qirshimi					
1970 19 Jan				Shaykh Khalifa ben Sulayman			
5 Feb		Muhsin al-Aini					
29 May					Shaykh Khalifa ben Hamad		
2 Aug						Saiyyid Tariq ben Taimur	
1971 3 May		Ahmad Muhammad Noman					
24 Aug		General Hassan al-Amri					
18 Sept		Muhsin al-Aini					
9 Dec							Shaykh Maktum ben Rashid al-Maktum
1972 2 Jan						Sultan Qabus	
30 Dec		Abdullah al-Hajari					

MINISTERS OF FOREIGN AFFAIRS

FOR (A)

		EGYPT	SYRIA	LEBANON	IRAQ	TRANS-JORDAN
1900	1 Jan	Boutros Ghali Pasha				
1910	22 Feb	Husayn Rushdi Pasha				
1912	15 Apr	Yusuf Wahba Pasha				
1914	5 Apr	Adli Yeghen Pasha				
	17 Dec	*None (Note 33)*				
1920	8 Mar		Said al-Husayni			
	3 May		Abd al-Rahman al-Shahbandar			
	25 July		*None (Note 1)*			
1922	1 Mar	Abd al-Khalek Sarwat Pasha				
	30 Nov	Mahmud Fakhri Pasha				
1923	15 Mar	Ahmad Hishmet Pasha				
	6 Aug	Tawfiq Rifaat Pasha				
1924	28 Jan	Wasif Boutros Ghali Effendi				
	2 Aug				Yasin al-Hashimi	
	24 Nov	Ahmad Ziwer Pasha				
1925	26 June				Abd al-Muhsin al-Sa'dun	
1926	7 June	Abd al-Khalek Sarwat Pasha				
	21 Nov				General Ja'far Pasha al-Askari	
1927	26 Apr	Morqos Hanna Pasha				
1928	14 Jan				Abd al-Muhsin al-Sa'dun	
	16 Mar	Wasif Boutros Ghali Pasha				

FOR (A)

	EGYPT	SYRIA	LEBANON	IRAQ	TRANS-JORDAN
	Ghali	*None*		al-Sa'dun	
1928 27 June	Dr Hafiz al-Afifi Bey				
1929 28 Apr				Tawfiq Bey al-Suwaydi	
19 Sept				Abd al-Muhsin al-Sa'dun	
4 Oct	Ahmad Midhat Yeghen Pasha				
1930 1 Jan	Wasif Boutros Ghali Pasha				
23 Mar				General Nuri Pasha al-Said	
20 June	Dr Hafiz al-Afifi Bey				
15 July	Abd al-Fatah Yahya Pasha				
27 Oct				Dr Abdallah Bey al-Damluji	
1931 19 Oct				General Ja'far Pasha al-Askari	
1932 3 Nov				Abd al-Kader Rashid	
1933 4 Jan	Nakhlah al-Muti Pasha				
20 Mar				General Nuri Pasha al-Said	
9 July	Salib Bey Samih				
21 Sept	Abd al-Fatah Yahya Pasha				
1934 21 Feb				Dr Abdallah Bey al-Damluji	
19 July				Tawfiq Bey al-Suwaydi	
27 Aug				General Nuri Pasha al-Said	

FOR (A)

	EGYPT	SYRIA	LEBANON	IRAQ	TRANS-JORDAN
	Yahya	*None*		al-Said	
1934 15 Nov	Kamil Bey Ibrahim				
1935 18 Feb	Abd al-Aziz Izzet Pasha				
1936 30 Jan	Ali Mahir Pasha				
9 May	Wasif Boutros Ghali Pasha				
30 Oct				Naji al-Asil	
21 Dec		Sa'd Allah al-Jabiri			
1937 10 July			Amir Khalid Abu al-Lam		
17 Aug				Tawfiq al-Suwaydi	
31 Oct			Khair al-Din al-Ahdab		
29 Dec	Abd al-Fatah Yahya Pasha				
1938 18 Mar			Selim Taqla		
24 Oct			Hamid Franjiyeh		
25 Dec				General Nuri Pasha al-Said	
1939 22 Jan			Habib Abu Shahla		
23 Feb		Fa'iz al-Khuri			
6 Apr		Khalid Pasha al-Azm			
26 Apr				Ali Jawdat	
11 July		*None* (Note 21)			
6 Aug					Tawfiq Pasha Abu al-Huda
18 Aug	Ali Mahir Pasha				
21 Sept			*None* (Note 22)		
1940 22 Feb				General Nuri Pasha al-Said	

FOR (A)

	EGYPT	SYRIA	LEBANON	IRAQ	TRANS-JORDAN
	Ali Mahir	*None*	*None*	Nuri al-Said	Abu al-Huda
1940 28 June	Hassan Sabri Pasha				
15 Nov	Husayn Sirri Pasha				
1941 21 Jan				Ali Mahmud al-Shaykh	
3 Feb				General Taha Pasha al-Hashimi	
4 Feb				Tawfiq al-Suwaydi	
13 Apr				Musa Bey al-Shahbandar	
4 June				Ali Jawdat	
27 June	Salib Samih Pasha				
21 Sept		Fa'iz al-Khuri			
10 Oct				Salih Jabir	
1 Dec			Hamid Franjiyeh		
1942 6 Feb	Mustafa Nahas Pasha				
11 Feb				Dr Abdallah al-Damluji	
3 July				General Nuri Pasha al-Said	
July			Philippe Bulos		
9 Oct				Abd al-Illah al-Hafiz	
1943 22 Mar			Jawad Bulos		
25 Mar		Naim Bey al-Antaki			
24 June				Nasrat al-Farisi	
18 Aug		Jamil Bey Mardam			
25 Sept			Salim Taqla		
Oct				Tahsin* al-Askari	

FOR (A)

	EGYPT	SYRIA	LEBANON	IRAQ	TRANS-JORDAN
	Nahas	Mardam	Taqla	al-Askari	Abu al-Huda
1943 25 Dec				Mahmud Subhi al-Daftari	
1944 4 June				Arshad al-Umari	
9 Oct	Mahmud Fahmy al-Nuqrashi Pasha				
1945 15 Jan			Henri Pharaon		
7 Mar	Abd al-Hamid Badawi Pasha				
23 Aug			Hamid Franjiyeh		
27 Aug		Mikhail Liyan			
Oct		Sa'd Allah al-Jabiri			
1946 17 Feb	Ahmad Lutfi al-Saiyid Pasha				
23 Feb				Tawfiq al-Suwaydi	
22 May			Abi Chahla		
23 May				Ali Mumtaz	
1 June				Muhammad Fadil Jamali	
12 Sept	Ibrahim Abd al-Hadi Pasha				
10 Dec	Mahmud Fahmy al-Nuqrashi Pasha				
15 Dec			Henri Pharaon		
28 Dec		Naim Bey al-Antaki			
1947 6 Feb					Samir Pasha al-Rifai
17 Apr		Khalid Bey Mardam			
8 June			Hamid Franjiyeh		
19 Nov	Ahmad Muhammad Khashaba Pasha				

FOR (A)

	EGYPT	SYRIA	LEBANON	IRAQ	TRANS-JORDAN
	Khashaba	Mardam	Franjiyeh	Jamali	al-Rifai
1947 31 Dec					Dr Fawzi Pasha Mulqi
1948 29 Jan				Hamdi al-Pachachi	
27 Mar				Nasrat al-Farisi	
26 June				Muzahim al-Pachachi	
23 Aug		Muhsin al-Barazi			
16 Dec		Khalid Pasha al-Azm			
28 Dec	Ibrahim Dassuqi Abaza Pasha				
1949 6 Jan				Abd al-Illah al-Hafiz	
27 Feb	Ahmad Muhammad Khashaba Pasha				
18 Mar				Muhammad Fadil Jamali	
17 Apr		Adil Arslan			
7 May					Ruhi Bey Abd al-Hadi
26 July	Husayn Sirri Pasha				
17 Aug		Nazim al-Qudsi			
Sept				Shaikir al-Wadi	
1 Oct			Philippe Taqla		
10 Dec				Muzahim al-Pachachi	
27 Dec		Khalid Pasha al-Azm			
1950 12 Jan	Muhammad Salah al-Din				
5 Feb				Tawfiq al-Suwaydi	
13 Apr					Muhammad Pasha Shurayqi
8 Sept		Nazim al-Qudsi			
16 Sept				Shaikir* al-Wadi	

32

FOR (A)

	EGYPT	SYRIA	LEBANON	IRAQ	JORDAN
	Salah al-Din	al-Qudsi	Taqla	al-Wadi	Shurayqi
1950 14 Oct					Ruhi Pasha Abd al-Hadi
4 Dec					Samir Pasha al-Rifai
1951 6 Feb				Tawfiq* al-Suwaydi	
13 Feb			Husayn al-Uwayni		
1 Mar					Ahmad Bey Tuqan
27 Mar		Khalid Pasha al-Azm			
17 Apr					Anastas Hananiyah
7 June			Charles Hilu		
25 July					Tawfiq Pasha Abu al-Huda
9 Aug		Faydi al-Atasi			
28 Nov		Shakir al-As			
3 Dec		*None (Note 21)*			
1952 27 Jan	Ali Mahir Pasha				
11 Feb			Philippe Taqla		
2 Mar	Abd al-Khalek Hassouna Pasha				
9 June		Zafir Rifai			
2 July	Husayn Sirri Pasha				
12 July				Muhammad Fadil Jamali	
22 July	Abd al-Khalek Hassouna Pasha				
23 July	Ali Mahir Pasha				
7 Sept	Ahmad Farag Tayyi				
10 Sept			Nazim Akkari		

FOR (A)

	EGYPT	SYRIA	LEBANON	IRAQ	JORDAN
	Tayyi	Rifai	Akkari	Jamali	Abu al-Huda
1952 1 Oct			Musa Mubarak		
8 Dec	Mahmud Fawzi				
1953 29 Jan				Tawfiq al-Suwaydi	
1 May			Georges Hakim		
5 May					Husayn al-Khalidi
19 July		Khalil Mardam			
13 Aug			Alfred Naqqash		
17 Sept				Abdallah Bakr	
1954 1 Mar		Faydi al-Atasi			
8 Mar				Musa al-Shahbandar	
29 Apr				Muhammad Fadil Jamali	
4 May					Jamal Tuqan
19 June		Izzat Sakal			
4 Aug				Musa al-Shahbandar	
24 Oct					Walid Salah
3 Nov		Faydi al-Atasi			
1955 13 Feb		Khalid Pasha al-Azm			
8 May				Burhan al-Din Bashayan	
30 May					Said al-Mufti
9 July			Hamid Franjiyeh		
13 Sept		Said al-Ghazzi			
19 Sept			Salim Lahud		
15 Dec					Haza' al-Majali
20 Dec					Samir al-Rifai
1956 9 Jan					Husayn al-Khalidi
22 May					Fawzi al-Mufti

FOR (A)

	EGYPT	SYRIA	LEBANON	IRAQ	JORDAN
	Fawzi	al-Ghazzi	Lahud	Bashayan	al-Mufti
1956 14 June		Salah al-Din Bitar			
1 July					Awni Abd al-Hadi
29 Oct					Sulayman al-Nabulsi
27 Nov			Charles Malik		
1957 25 Apr					Samir al-Rifai
20 June				Ali Jawdat	
15 Dec				Burhan al-Din Bashayan	
1958 3 Mar				Muhammad Fadil Jamali	
6 Mar		Mahmud Fawzi *(Note 26)*			
18 May				Tawfiq al-Suwaydi *(Note 34)*	
14 July				Abd al-Jabbar al-Jumard	
24 Sept			Philippe Taqla		
14 Oct			Husayn al-Uwayni		
1959 7 Feb				Hashim Jawwad	
6 May					Haza' al-Majali
20 Sept					Musa Nasir
1960 14 May			Philippe Taqla		
1961 28 June					Bahjat al-Talhouni
30 Sept		Dr Ma'mun Kuzbari			
11 Nov					Rafiq al-Husayni
20 Nov		Izzat al-Nus			
22 Dec		Ma'ruf al-Dawalibi			
1962 27 Jan					Hazem Nusaybeh
16 Apr		Dr Adnan al-Azhari			
20 June		Jamal al-Farah			
17 Sept		Asad Muhasin			

FOR (A)

	EGYPT	SYRIA	LEBANON	IRAQ	JORDAN
	Fawzi	Muhasin	Taqla	Jawwad	Nusaybeh
1963 8 Feb				Talib Husayn Shabib	
9 Mar		Salah al-Din Bitar			
21 Apr					Amin Yunis al-Husayni
10 July					Sharif Husayn ben Nasr
31 Oct					Antun Atallah
12 Nov		Hassan Muraywad			
20 Nov				Colonel Subhi Abd al-Hamid	
1964 25 Mar	Dr Mahmud Riad *(Note 35)*				
1 Apr			Fuad Ammun		
7 July					Kadri Tuqan
14 Nov				Naji Talib	
18 Nov			Philippe Taqla		
1965 13 Feb					Hazem Nusaybeh
2 June			Husayn al-Uwayni		
25 July			Georges Hakim		
6 Sept				Abd al-Rahman al-Bazzaz	
23 Sept		Dr Ibrahim Makhous			
1966 1 Jan		Salah al-Din Bitar			
12 Feb					Akram Zuwaytar
1 Mar		Dr Ibrahim Makhous			
9 Apr			Philippe Taqla		
18 Apr				Dr Adnan al-Pachachi	
7 Dec			Georges Hakim		
22 Dec					Abdallah Salah
1967 23 Apr					Ahmad Tuqan

FOR (A)

	EGYPT	SYRIA	LEBANON	IRAQ	JORDAN
	Riad	Makhous	Hakim	al-Pachachi	Tuqan
1967 10 July				Ismail* Khayrallah	
2 Aug					Muhammad Adib Amiri
7 Oct					Bahjat al-Talhouni
1968 8 Feb			Fuad Butros		
25 Apr					Abd al-Moneim Rifai
17 July				Dr Nasr al-Hani	
31 July				Abd al-Karim Shaikli	
12 Oct			Ali Arab		
20 Oct			Husayn al-Uwayni		
29 Oct		Muhammad Ashawi			
1969 15 Jan			Rashid Karami		
23 Jan			Yusef Salam		
24 Mar					Ahmad Tuqan
8 Apr		Mustafa al-Saiyyid			
12 Aug					Abd al-Moneim Rifai
25 Nov			Nassim Majdalani		
1970 27 June					Antun Atallah
16 Sept					Brigadier Muhammad Daoud
26 Sept					Ahmad Tuqan
13 Oct			Khalil Abu Hamad		
28 Oct					Abdallah Salah
21 Nov		Abd al-Halim Khaddam			
1971 19 Sept	Dr Muhammad Murad Ghaleb *(Note 36)*				
30 Sept				Rashid Rifai	
30 Oct				Murtada al-Hadithi	

FOR (A)

	EGYPT	SYRIA	LEBANON	IRAQ	JORDAN
	Ghaleb	Khaddam	Abu Hamad	al-Hadithi	Salah
1972 21 Aug					Salah Abu Zeid
8 Sept	Dr Muhammad Hassan al-Zayyat				

MINISTERS OF FOREIGN AFFAIRS

FOR (B)

	MOROCCO	ALGERIA	TUNISIA	LIBYA	SUDAN	SOUTHERN YEMEN
1951 29 Mar				Ali Bey al-Jarbi		
24 Dec				Mahmud Muntasir		
1954 18 Feb				Muhammad al-Saghisli		
12 Apr				Abd al-Salim al-Busayri		
1956 2 Feb					Mubarak Zarrouk	
26 Mar				Mustafa ben Halim		
14 Apr			Habib Bourguiba			
26 Apr	Ahmad Balafrej					
7 July					Muhammad Ahmad Mahgoub	
31 Oct				Ali Sahili		
1957 26 May				Wahbi al-Buri		
29 July			Sadok Mokkadem			
1958 19 Sept		Dr Muhammad Lamine Debaghine *(Note 30)*				
13 Oct				Abd al-Majid Qubar		
18 Nov					Ahmad Khayir	
24 Dec	Abdallah Ibrahim					
1960 19 Jan		Krim Belkacem *(Note 30)*				
26 May	Driss Mhammedi					
17 Oct				Abd al-Qadir al-Allam		
Oct	Abd al-Karim Benjelloun					
1961 25 Jan	Muhammad Boucetta					
4 May				Sulayman al-Jarbi		
10 June	King Hassan II					
27 Aug		Sa'd Dahlab *(Note 30)*				
21 Dec	Ahmad Balafrej					
1962 28 Jan				Wanis al-Qadafi		

FOR (B)

	MOROCCO	ALGERIA	TUNISIA	LIBYA	SUDAN	SOUTHERN YEMEN
	Balafrej	Sa'd Dahlab	Mokkadem	al-Qadafi	Khayir	
1962 15 Aug			Mongi Slim			
28 Sept		Muhammad Khemisti				
1963 6 Mar				Muhammad Atiyyat Abu Nuwaira		
19 Mar				Muhi al-Din Fikini		
5 May		*None*				
5 Sept		Abd al-Aziz Bouteflika				
13 Nov	Ahmad Reda Guedira					
1964 22 Jan				Husayn Mazik		
17 Aug	Ahmad Taybi Benhima					
30 Oct					Muhammad Ahmad Mahgoub	
11 Nov			Habib Bourguiba junior			
1965 18 Mar				Wahbi al-Buri		
17 June					Muhammad Ibrahim Khalil	
2 Oct				Ahmad al-Bishti		
1966 24 Feb	Muhammad Cherkaoui					
18 Apr					Muhammad Ahmad Mahgoub	
4 Aug					Ibrahim al-Mufti	
1967 11 Mar	Ahmad Laraki					
27 May					Muhammad Ahmad Mahgoub	
1 Dec						Sayf Ahmad Dhalai
1968 4 Jan				Wanis al-Qadafi		
2 June					Ali Abd al-Rahman	
4 Sept				Shams al-Din al-Arabi		

FOR (B)

	MOROCCO	ALGERIA	TUNISIA	LIBYA	SUDAN	SOUTHERN YEMEN
	Laraki	Bouteflika	Bourguiba junior	al-Arabi	Abd al-Rahman	Dhalai
1969 12 Feb						Faysal Abd al-Latif
25 May					Babikr Awadhallah	
9 June				Ali Hasanain		
1969 23 June						Ali Salim al-Baydh
8 Sept				Salih Buwaisir		
7 Oct	Abd al-Hadi Boutaleb					
1970 12 June			Muhammad Masmoudi			
21 July					General Jaafar al-Nimeiri	
22 Aug					Faruq Abu Isa	
16 Sept				Captain Muhammad Najm		
12 Oct	Dr Yusuf Bel Arabi Taarji					
8 Dec				*None*		
1971 31 Jan						Muhammad Ali Haitham
2 Aug						Muhammad Salih al-Aulaqi
3 Aug					Dr Mansur Khalid	
6 Aug	Abd al-Latif al-Filali					
1972 24 May	Ahmad Taib Benhima					
16 July				Mansur Rashid Kikhya		

FOR (C) MINISTERS OF FOREIGN AFFAIRS

	SAUDI ARABIA	YEMEN	KUWAIT	BAHRAIN	QATAR	OMAN	UNION OF ARAB EMIRATES
1953 9 Oct	Prince Faysal ben Abd al-Aziz (Note 37)						
1955 31 Aug		Crown Prince Muhammad al-Badr ben Ahmad (Note 38)					
1960 21 Dec	Shaykh Ibrahim al-Suwwayil						
1962 17 Jan			Shaykh Sabah al-Salim				
15 Mar	Crown Prince Faysal ben Abd al-Aziz (Note 39)						
19 Sept		Hassan Ibrahim					
28 Sept		Muhsin al-Aini					
31 Oct		Abd al-Rahman al-Baydani					
1963 31 Jan			Shaykh Sabah al-Ahmad				
18 Feb		President Abdallah al-Sallal					
25 Apr		Mustafa Yaqub					
1964 10 Feb		Hassan Makki					
3 May		Muhsin al-Sirri					
1965 6 Jan		Abd al-Qawi al-Hamim					
24 Apr		Muhsin al-Aini					
11 July		*None*					
20 July		Mustafa Yaqub					
1966 16 Apr		Hassan Makki					
18 Sept		Muhammad Abd al-Aziz Salam					
1967 12 Oct		President Abdallah al-Sallal					
5 Nov		Hassan Makki					
1968 15 Sept		Yahia Jughman					
1969 3 Apr		Husayn Ali al-Hubayshi (Note 40)					

FOR (C)

	SAUDI ARABIA	YEMEN	KUWAIT	BAHRAIN	QATAR	OMAN	UNION OF ARAB EMIRATES
	Faysal	al-Hubayshi	Sabah al-Ahmad				
1969 2 Sept		Yahia Jughman *(Note 40)*					
1970 19 Jan				Shaykh Muhammad ben Mubarak			
5 Feb		Muhsin al-Aini					
2 Aug						Saiyyid Tariq Ben Taimur	
1971 3 May		Ahmad Muhammad Noman					
24 Aug		Abdallah Abd al-Majid al-Asnag					
18 Sept		Muhsin al-Aini					
9 Dec							Ahmad Khalifa al-Suwaydi
1972 2 Jan						Fahd Mahmoud	
22 Feb					Shaykh Suhaim ben Hamad		
30 Dec		Muhammad Ahmad Noman					

MINISTERS OF WAR/DEFENCE

WAR (A)

	EGYPT	SYRIA	LEBANON	IRAQ	TRANS-JORDAN
1900 1 Jan	Abani Pasha				
1908 12 Nov	Ismail Sirri Pasha				
1919 Mar	*None*				
9 Apr	Hassan Hassit Pasha				
12 Apr	*None*				
21 May	Ismail Sirri Pasha				
1920 8 Mar		Abd al-Hamid al-Qaltaqchi			
3 May		Yusuf al-Adhma			
20 May	Muhammad Shafik Pasha				
25 July		*None (Note 1)*			
11 Nov				General Ja'far Pasha al-Askari	
1921 24 May	Ibrahim Fathi Pasha				
1922 20 Nov				General Nuri Pasha al-Said	
30 Nov	Mahmud Azmi Pasha				
1924 28 Jan	Hassan Hassib Pasha				
27 July				Salih Bash Ayan	
2 Aug				General Yasin Pasha al-Hashimi	
24 Nov	Muhammad Sadiq Yahya Pasha				
1925 13 Mar	General Musa Fuad Pasha				
26 June				Sabih Bey Nashat	
1926 7 June	Ahmad Muhammad Khashaba Bey				

45

WAR (A)

	EGYPT	SYRIA	LEBANON	IRAQ	TRANS-JORDAN
	Khashaba	*None*		Nashat	
1926 21 Nov				General Nuri Pasha al-Said	
1927 26 Apr	Gaafar Wali Pasha				
1928 12 Jan				*None*	
9 June				General Nuri Pasha al-Said	
1929 29 Apr				Amin Bey Zaki	
19 Sept				General Nuri Pasha al-Said	
4 Oct	Muhammad Iflatun Pasha				
1930 1 Jan	Hassan Hassib Pasha				
23 Mar				General Ja'far Pasha al-Askari	
20 June	Muhammad Tawfiq Rifaat Pasha				
2 Nov				General Nuri Pasha al-Said	
1931 8 Jan				Jamil Pasha al-Rawi	
20 June	Ali Gamal al-Din Pasha				
19 Oct				General Ja'far Pasha al-Askari	
1932 3 Nov				Rashid Bey al-Khojah	
1933 20 Mar				Jelal Bey Baban	
21 Sept	Salib Samih Bey				

WAR (A)

	EGYPT	SYRIA	LEBANON	IRAQ	TRANS-JORDAN
	Samih	*None*		Baban	
1933 9 Nov				General Nuri Pasha al-Said	
1934 21 Feb				Rashid Bey al-Khojah	
27 Aug				Jamil al-Midfa'i	
15 Nov	General Muhammad Tawfiq Abdallah Bey				
1935 5 Mar				Rashid Bey al-Khojah	
17 Mar				General Ja'far Pasha al-Askari	
1936 30 Jan	Brigadier Ali Sidqi Pasha				
9 May	Brigadier Ali Fahmy Pasha				
30 Oct				Brigadier Abd al-Latif Nuri	
21 Dec		Shukri Bey al-Quwatli			
1937 12 Mar			Habib Abu Shahla		
10 July			Amir Khalid Abu al-Lam		
31 July	Ahmad Hamdi Sayf al-Nasr Pasha				
17 Aug				Jamil al-Midfa'i	
31 Oct			Musa Nammur		
29 Dec	General Husayn Rifqi Pasha				
1938 21 Mar		Jamil Bey Mardam			
27 Apr	Hassan Sabri Pasha				

WAR (A)

	EGYPT	SYRIA	LEBANON	IRAQ	TRANS-JORDAN
	Sabri	Mardam	Nammur	al-Midfa'i	
1938 24 Oct			Khalil Kuseib		
2 Nov				Subhi Najib Bey al-Izzi	
25 Dec				General Taha Pasha al-Hashimi	
1939 17 Jan	Husayn Sirri Pasha				
22 Jan			Habib Abu Shahla		
23 Feb		Mazhar Raslan			
6 Apr		Nasuhi al-Bukhari			
11 July		*None (Note 21)*			
6 Aug					Rashid Pasha al-Midfai
18 Aug	Muhammad Salih Harb Pasha				
21 Sept			*None (Note 22)*		
1940 28 June	Mahmud Fahmy Qaisi Pasha				
15 Nov	Yunus Salih Pasha				
27 Nov	Husayn Sirri Pasha				
5 Dec	Hassan Sadiq Bey				
1941 13 Apr				Naji Bey Shawkat	
9 June				Nazif al-Shawi	
30 July					Tawfiq Pasha Abu al-Huda
21 Sept		Amir Abd al-Ghaffar al-Atrash			
11 Oct				General Nuri Pasha al-Said	

WAR (A)

	EGYPT	SYRIA	LEBANON	IRAQ	TRANS-JORDAN
	Sadiq	al-Atrash	*None*	al-Said	Abu al-Huda
1941 1 Dec			Hikmat Jumblatt		
1942 6 Feb	Ahmad Hamdi Sayf al-Nasr Pasha				
27 Apr		Amir Hassan al-Atrash			
July			Ahmad al-Huzayni		
1943 25 Mar		Ata Bey al-Ayyubi			
18 Aug		Nasuhi al-Bukhari			
25 Sept			Amir Majid Arslan		
1944 4 June				Taha Ali	
30 Aug				Arshad al-Umari	
9 Oct	Saiyyid Salim				
14 Oct		Jamil Bey Mardam			
Dec				General Ismail Namiq	
1945 10 Jan			Abd al-Hamid Karami		
19 May					Ibrahim Pasha Hashim
27 Aug		Khalid Pasha al-Azm			
23 Aug			Ahmad al-Asad		
1 Oct		Sa'd Allah al-Jabiri			
1946 17 Feb	General Ahmad Atiyah Pasha				
22 May			*None listed*		
1 June				Said Haqqi	
21 Nov				Shaikir al-Wadi	
15 Dec			Amir Majid Arslan		
28 Dec		Ahmad Sharabati			

WAR (A)

	EGYPT	SYRIA	LEBANON	IRAQ	JORDAN
	Atiyah	Sharabati	Arslan	al-Wadi	Hashim
1947 6 Feb					Samir Pasha al-Rifa'i
19 Nov	General Muhammad Haidar Pasha				
1948 29 Jan				Arshad al-Umari	
23 May		Jamil Bey Mardam			
26 June				Sadiq al-Bassam	
20 Oct				Shaikir al-Wadi	
16 Dec		Khalid Pasha al-Azm			
1949 17 Apr		General Husni al-Zaim			
7 May					Fawzi al-Mulqi *(Note 41)*
17 Aug		General Abdallah Atfah			
10 Dec				Umar al-Nazmi	
24 Dec		Faydi al-Atassi			
27 Dec		Akram al-Hawrani			
1950 12 Jan	Mustafa Nasrat Bey				
5 Feb				Shaikir al-Wadi	
4 June		Colonel Fawzi Silo			
4 Dec					Umar Bey Matar
1951 13 Feb			Husayn al-Uwayni		
7 June			Rashid Baydun		
25 July					Sulayman Bey Tuqan
28 Nov		Dr Ma'ruf al-Dawalibi			
3 Dec		Colonel Fawzi Silo			

WAR (A)

	EGYPT	SYRIA	LEBANON	IRAQ	JORDAN
	Nasrat	Silo	Baydun	al-Wadi	Tuqan
1952 27 Jan	Ali Mahir Pasha				
11 Feb			Amir Majid Arslan		
2 Mar	Murtada al-Maraghi Bey				
2 July	Husayn Sirri Pasha				
12 July				Husam al-Din Juma	
22 July	Colonel Ismail Sharin Bey				
24 July	Ali Mahir Pasha				
7 Sept	General Muhammad Neguib				
10 Sept			Nazim Akkari		
18 Sept			General Fuad Shihab		
24 Sept					Tawfiq Pasha Abu al-Huda
1 Oct			Salim Haydar		
23 Nov				General Nur al-Din Mahmud	
1953 29 Jan				General Nuri Pasha al-Said	
1 May			Saeb Salem		
5 May					Fawzi al-Mulqi
18 June	Abd al-Latif al-Baghdadi				
19 July		General Rifaat Khankan			
13 Aug			Abdallah al-Yafi		
17 Sept				General Husayn Makki Khammas	

WAR (A)

	EGYPT	SYRIA	LEBANON	IRAQ	JORDAN
	al-Baghdadi	Khankan	al-Yafi	Khammas	al-Mulqi
1954 1 Mar		Dr Ma'ruf al-Dawalibi	Amir Majid Arslan		
18 Apr	Colonel Husayn al-Shafai				
4 May					Anwar Nusaybeh
19 June		Said al-Ghazzi			
4 Aug				General Nuri Pasha al-Said	
1 Sept	General Abd al-Hakim Amer				
3 Nov		Rashid Barmada			
1955 13 Feb		Khalid Pasha al-Azm			
30 May					Farhan al-Shubaylat
13 Sept		Rashid Barmada			
20 Dec					Fawzi al-Mulqi
1956 9 Jan					Falah al-Maladihah
22 May					Muhammad Ali al-Ajlani
14 June		Abd al-Hasib Raslan			
1 July					Umar Matar
29 Oct					Abd al-Halim Nimr
27 Nov			General Fuad Shihab		
1957 2 Jan		Khalid Pasha al-Azm			
3 Jan			Samih al-Sulh		
15 Apr					Husayn Fakhri al-Khalidi
25 Apr					Sulayman Tuqan
20 June				Ahmad Mukhtar Baban	

WAR (A)

	EGYPT	SYRIA	LEBANON	IRAQ	JORDAN
	Amer	al-Azm	al-Sulh	Baban	Tuqan
1957 18 Aug			Amir Majid Arslan		
15 Dec				Abd al-Wahhab Marjan	
1958 3 Mar				*General Nuri Pasha al-Said	
6 Mar		Field Marshal Abd al-Hakim Amer *(Note 26)*			
14 Mar			Rashid Baydun		
18 May				Sulayman Tuqan *(Note 42)*	
22 May			Samih al-Sulh		
14 July				General Abd al-Karim Qasim	
15 July					Samir al-Rifai
24 Sept			Rashid Karami		
1959 27 Jan					Ahmad al-Tarawnah
6 May					Anwar Nashashibi
20 Sept					Wasfi Mirza
1960 14 May			Ahmad al-Da'uq		
2 Aug			Amir Majid Arslan		
29 Aug					Aqif al-Fayiz
1961 27 Mar					Wasfi Mirza
19 May			Saeb Salem		
6 Sept					Hassan al-Katib
30 Sept		Dr Ma'mun Kuzbari			
31 Oct			Amir Majid Arslan		
5 Nov					Ahmad al-Tarawnah
20 Nov		Izzat al-Nus			

WAR (A)

	EGYPT	SYRIA	LEBANON	IRAQ	JORDAN
	Amer	al-Nus	Arslan	Qasim	al-Tarawnah
1961 22 Dec		Rashid Barmada			
1962 27 Jan					Wasfi al-Tall
16 Apr		Abd al-Karim Zahir al-Din			
29 Sept	Abd al-Wahhab al-Bishri				
1963 8 Feb				Salih Mahdi Ammash	
9 Mar		Colonel Muhammad Sufi			
27 Mar					Samir al-Rifai
21 Apr					Sharif Husayn ben Nasr
13 May		Ziyad al-Hariri			
10 July		General Amin al-Hafiz			Abd al-Qadir Salih
5 Aug		General Abdallah Ziyadah			
20 Nov				Air Marshal Hardan al-Takriti	
1964 20 Feb			Husayn al-Uwayni		
2 Mar				*General Tahir Yahya	
13 Mar		Memduh Jabir			
7 July					Nizam al-Sharabi
14 Nov				Muhsin al-Habib	
1965 13 Feb					Wasfi al-Tall
25 July			Rashid Karami		
6 Sept				Arif Abd al-Razzaq	
21 Sept				Abd al-Aziz al-Uqayli	
23 Sept		General Hamad Ubayd			
20 Dec			Michel Khuri		

WAR (A)

	EGYPT	SYRIA	LEBANON	IRAQ	JORDAN
	al-Bishri	Ubayd	Khuri	al-Uqayli	al-Tall
1966 1 Jan		General Muhammad Umran			
23 Feb		General Hafiz al-Assad			
9 Apr			Fuad Butros		
18 Apr				General Shakir Mahmud Shukri	
10 Sept	Shams al-Din Bedran				
7 Dec			Bedri al-Meouchi		
1967 4 Mar					Sharif Husayn ben Nasr
23 Apr					Saad Jumaa
19 June	Muhammad Abd al-Wahhab al-Bishri				
21 July	Hamid Amin Huweidi				
7 Oct					Field Marshal Habis al-Majali
1968 24 Jan	General Muhammad Fawzi				
8 Feb			Abdallah al-Yafi		
25 Apr					Bahjat al-Talhouni
3 July			Rashid Beydoun		
17 July				General Ibrahim Daoud	
31 July				Air Marshal Hardan al-Takriti	
12 Oct			Amir Majid Arslan		
20 Oct			Husayn al-Uwayni		
26 Dec					Ahmad Tuqan
1969 15 Jan			Amir Majid Arslan		

WAR (A)

	EGYPT	SYRIA	LEBANON	IRAQ	JORDAN
	Fawzi	al-A'ssad	Arslan	al-Takriti	Tuqan
1969 30 June					General Ammar Khammash
26 Aug					Ahmad Tuqan
1970 3 Apr				General Hammad Shihab	
19 Apr					General Ali al-Hayyari
27 June					Abd al-Wahhab al-Majali
16 Sept					General Mutlaq Id
26 Sept					General Akkash Zaban
13 Oct			Edouard Sawmah		
28 Oct					Wasfi al-Tall
18 Nov			*Elias Saba		
1971 3 Apr		Mutib Shunaiwi			
14 May	General Muhammad Sadiq				
29 Nov					Ahmad Lawzi
1972 23 Mar		General Mustafa Tlas			
27 May			Amir Majid Arslan		
26 Oct	General Ahmad Ismail				

MINISTERS OF WAR/DEFENCE

WAR (B)

	MOROCCO	ALGERIA	TUNISIA	LIBYA	SUDAN	SOUTHERN YEMEN
1951 29 Mar				Umar Shannib		
24 Dec				Ali al-Jarbi		
1954 9 Jan					Khalafallah Khalid	
18 Feb				Khalil al-Jalal		
19 Dec				Ibrahim ben Sha'ban		
25 Dec					Ismail al-Azhari	
1956 2 Feb					Abdallah Khalil	
22 Mar	Ahmad Reda Guedira					
26 Mar				Ali Jawdah		
14 Apr			Habib Bourguiba			
26 Oct	Muhammad Zeghari					
31 Oct				Abd al-Qadir al-Allam		
1957 26 May				Siddiq al-Muntasir		
29 July			Bahi Ladgham			
12 Sept	Ahmad Lyazidi					
1958 27 Apr				Ibrahim ben Sha'ban		
19 Sept		Krim Belkacem *(Note 30)*				
18 Nov					General Ibrahim Abboud	
24 Dec	Muhammad Awadh					
1960 19 Jan		*None*				
26 May	Crown Prince Hassan ben Muhammad					
17 Oct				Ahmad al-Hasairi		
1961 4 May				Yunis Abd al-Nabi Bilkhayr		
2 June	Mahjub Ahardan					
1962 28 Sept		Colonel Houari Boumedienne				
1963 19 Mar				Sayf al-Nasr Abd al-Jalil		
1964 29 July				Abd al-Salam Bsikri		

WAR (B)

	MOROCCO	ALGERIA	TUNISIA	LIBYA	SUDAN	SOUTHERN YEMEN
	Ahardan	Boumedienne	Ladgham	Bsikri	Abboud	
1964 20 Aug	General Muhammad Mazziane Zahraoui					
30 Oct					Sirr al-Khatim al-Khalifa	
1965 17 June					Muhammad Ahmad Mahgoub	
2 Oct				General Muhammad al-Mansuri		
1966 22 Feb	Mahjub Ahardan					
22 Mar				Yusuf Abu Sayf Yasin		
6 May					Amin al-Tom	
24 June			Ahmad Mestiri			
4 Aug					Abdallah Nagdallah	
14 Dec					Ahmad al-Mahdi	
1967 11 Mar	Muhammad Cherkaoui					
27 May					Muhammad* Ahmad Mahgoub	
6 July	Muhammad Haddou Chiguer					
July					Dr Adam Madibu	
25 Oct				Hamid Ubaydi		
1 Dec						Ali Salim al-Baydh
1968 29 Jan			Bahi Ladgham			
13 Apr			Muhammad M'zali			
20 Apr						Muhammad Salah al-Aulaqi
2 June					Muhammad Ahmad Mahgoub	
15 June	General Muhammad Mazziane Zahraoui					
1969 26 May					General Jaafar al-Nimeiri	

58

WAR (B)

	MOROCCO	ALGERIA	TUNISIA	LIBYA	SUDAN	SOUTHERN YEMEN
	Zahraoui	Boumedienne	M'zali	Ubaydi	al-Nimeiri	al-Aulaqi
1969 19 June					Umar al-Haj Musa	
8 Sept				Colonel Adam al-Hawwaz		
28 Oct					Brigadier Khalid Hassan Abbas	
7 Nov			Qaid Beji Essibsi			
10 Dec				Colonel Muammar al-Qadafi		
30 Dec						Ali Nasr Muhammad Hassani
1970 12 June			Hasib ben Ammar			
3 Oct	Muhammad Bahnini					
19 Aug	King Hassan II					
1971 6 Aug	General Muhammad Oufkir					
29 Oct			Bashir Mehedebi			
1972 13 Feb					General Jaafar al-Nimeiri	
9 Aug			Abdallah Farhat			
17 Aug	General Driss ben Omar al-Alami					

59

WAR (C)   MINISTERS OF WAR/DEFENCE

		SAUDI ARABIA	YEMEN	KUWAIT	BAHRAIN	QATAR	OMAN	UNION OF ARAB EMIRATES
1953	9 Oct	Prince Mishal ben Abd al-Aziz *(Note 31)*						
1955	31 Aug		Crown Prince Muhammad al-Badr ben Ahmad *(Note 32)*					
1956	26 Dec	Prince Fahad ben Saud						
1960	21 Dec	Prince Muhammad ben Saud *(Note 43)*						
1962	31 Jan			Shaykh Muhammad al-Ahmad				
	28 Sept		Hammud al-Jayifi					
	31 Oct	Prince Sultan ben Abd al-Aziz	Colonel Abdallah Jizaylan					
1963	25 Apr		Husayn al-Dafi'a					
1964	6 Dec			Shaikh Sa'd al-Abdallah				
1965	6 Jan		Muhammad al-Ahnumi					
	24 Apr		Muhammad al-Ra'ini					
1966	16 Apr		General Hammud al-Jayifi					
	18 Sept		President Abdallah al-Sallal					
1967	5 Nov		Colonel Abd al-Karim al-Sukkari					
	21 Dec		General Hassan al-Amri *(Note 44)*					
1970	19 Jan				Shaykh Hamad ben Isa			
	17 Aug						Colonel Hugh Oldman *(Note 45)*	
1971	5 Sept		*None*					

	SAUDI ARABIA	YEMEN	KUWAIT	BAHRAIN	QATAR	OMAN	UNION OF ARAB EMIRATES
	Sultan	*None*	Said	Hamad		Oldman	
1971 9 Dec							Shaykh Muhammad ben Rashid al-Maktum

WAR (C)

MINISTERS OF THE INTERIOR

INT (A)

		EGYPT	SYRIA	LEBANON	IRAQ	TRANS-JORDAN
1900	1 Jan	Mustafa Fahmy Pasha				
1908	12 Nov	Muhammad Said Pasha				
1914	5 Apr	Husayn Rushdi Pasha				
1919	Mar	*None*				
	9 Apr	Adli Yeghen Pasha				
	23 Apr	*None*				
	21 May	Muhammad Said Pasha				
	19 Nov	Muhammad Tawfiq Nasim Pasha				
1920	8 Mar		Rida al-Sulh			
	3 May		Hashim al-Atasi			
	25 July		*None (Note 1)*			
	11 Nov				Saiyyid Talib Pasha al-Naqib	
1921	16 Mar	Abd al-Khalek Sarwat Pasha				
	Apr				Hajji Ramzi Bey	
1922	3 Mar				Tawfiq al-Khlaidi	
	25 Oct				Abd al-Muhsin al-Sa'dun	
	20 Nov				Naji Bey al-Suwaydi	
	29 Nov				Abd al-Muhsin al-Sa'dun	
	30 Nov	Muhammad Tawfiq Nasim Pasha				
1923	15 Mar	Yahya Ibrahim Pasha				
	22 Nov				Ali Jawdat	
1924	28 Jan	Sa'd Zaghlul Pasha				

INT (A)

		EGYPT	SYRIA	LEBANON	IRAQ	TRANS-JORDAN
		Zaghlul	*None*		Jawdat	
1924	2 Aug				Abd al-Muhsin al-Sa'dun	
	24 Nov	Ahmad Ziwer Pasha				
	9 Dec	Ismail Sidqi Pasha				
1925	Jan		Nasri al-Bakhhash			
	26 June				Rashid Ali al-Gaylani	
	July				Hikmat Sulayman	
	12 Sept	Muhammad Hilmi Isa Pasha				
	3 Dec	Ahmad Ziwer Pasha				
	21 Dec		*None (Note 2)*			
1926	4 May		Husni Bey al-Barazi			
	31 May			Bishara Bey al-Khuri		
	7 June	Adli Yeghen Pasha				
	17 June				Abd al-Aziz al-Qassab	
	12 June		Wathiq Bey al-Muayyad			
	1 July					Hassan Khalid Pasha Abu al-Huda
	21 Nov				Rashid Ali al-Gaylani	
	6 Dec		Rauf Bey al-Ayyubi			
1927	26 Apr	Abd al-Khalek Sarwat Pasha				
	5 May			Georges Thabit		
1928	5 Jan			Ayyub Thabit		
	11 Jan				Abd al-Aziz al-Qassab	

INT (A)

		EGYPT	SYRIA	LEBANON	IRAQ	TRANS-JORDAN
		Sarwat	al-Ayyubi	Thabit	al-Qassab	Abu al-Huda
1928	15 Feb		Said Bey al-Muhaysin			
	16 Mar	Mustafa Nahas Pasha				
	9 June				Naji Bey Shawkat	
	27 June	Muhammad Mahmud Pasha				
	10 Aug			Musa Nammur		
1929	29 Apr				Abd al-Aziz al-Qassab	
	9 May			Bishara Bey al-Khuri		
	19 Sept				Naji Bey Suwaydi	
	4 Oct	Adli Yeghen Pasha				
	11 Oct			Emile Eddé		
	18 Nov				Naji Bey Shawkat	
1930	1 Jan	Mustafa Nahas Pasha				
	23 Mar				Jamil al-Midfa'i	
	25 Mar			Musa Nammur		
	10 June		Jamil al-Ulshi			
	30 June	Ismail Sidqi Pasha				
1931	6 Jan				General Nuri Pasha al-Said	
					Muzahim Bey al-Pachachi	
	19 Oct				Naji Bey Shawkat	
	Nov		*None (Note 2)*			
1932	May			*None (Note 2)*		
	7 June		Haqqi al-Azm Pasha			

65

INT (A)

		EGYPT	SYRIA	LEBANON	IRAQ	TRANS-JORDAN
		Sidqi	al-Azm	*None*	Shawkat	Abu al-Huda
1933	13 Mar	Mahmud Fahmy al-Qaysi Pasha				
	20 Mar				Hikmat Bey Sulayman	
	9 Nov				Naji Bey Shawkat	
1934	21 Feb				Jamil al-Midfa'i	
	16 Mar		Shaykh Taj al-Din al-Hasani			
	27 Aug				Ali Jawdat	
	15 Nov	Muhammad Tawfiq Nasim Pasha				
1935	5 Mar				Abd al-Aziz al-Qassab	
	17 Mar				Rashid Ali al-Gaylani	
1936	30 Jan	Ali Mahir Pasha				
	22 Feb		Ata Bey al-Ayyubi			
	9 May	Mustafa Nahas Pasha				
	30 Oct				Hikmat Sulayman	
	21 Dec		Sa'd Allah al-Jabiri			
1937	5 Jan			Khair al-Din al-Ahdab		
	13 Mar			Michel Zakkur		
	10 July			Habib Abu Shahla		
	17 Aug				Mustafa Bey al-Umari	
	29 Dec	Muhammad Mahmud Pasha				
1938	18 Mar			Joseph Stephane		
	18 May	Ahmad Lutfi al-Saiyid Pasha				

INT (A)

		EGYPT	SYRIA	LEBANON	IRAQ	TRANS-JORDAN
		al-Saiyid	al-Jabiri	Stephane	al-Umari	Abu al-Huda
1938	24 June	Mahmud Fahmy al-Nuqrashi Pasha				
	24 Oct			Khalil Kuseib		
	2 Nov				Jamil al-Midfa'i	
	25 Dec				Naji Shawkat	
1939	22 Jan			Habib Abu Shahla		
	23 Feb		Muzhir Raslan			
	26 Apr				General Nuri Pasha al-Said	
	6 Apr		Nasuhi al-Bukhari			
	10 July		Bahij al-Khatib			
	6 Aug					Rashid Pasha al-Midfai
	18 Aug	Ali Mahir Pasha				
	21 Sept			*None (Note 22)*		
	22 Sept				Umar al-Nazmi	
1940	31 Mar				Rashid Ali al-Gaylani	
	28 June	Mahmud Fahmy al-Nuqrashi Pasha				
	31 Aug	Hassan Sabri Pasha				
	15 Nov	Husayn Sirri Pasha				
1941	3 Feb				Umar al-Nazmi	
	4 Apr		Khalid Pasha al-Azm			
	7 Apr			Alfred Naqqash		
	13 Apr				Rashid Ali al-Gaylani	
	4 June				Mustafa al-Umari	

67

INT (A)

	EGYPT	SYRIA	LEBANON	IRAQ	TRANS-JORDAN
	Sirri	al-Azm	Naqqash	al-Umari	al-Midfai
1941 21 Sept		Bahij al-Khatib			
10 Oct				Salih Jabir	
1 Dec			Ahmad al-Husayni		
1942 6 Feb	Mustafa Nahas Pasha				
19 Apr		Husni al-Barazi			
10 July			Hikmat Jumblatt		
8 Oct				Tahsin al-Askari	
10 Dec					Arif Bey al-Anabtawi
1943 10 Jan		Jamil al-Ulshi			
22 Mar			Ayyub Thabit		
25 Mar		Ata Bey al-Ayyubi			
1 June	Fuad Serag al-Din Pasha				
23 June				Salih Jabir	
1 Aug			Tawfiq Awad		
19 Aug		Lutfi Haffar			
25 Sept			Camille Chamoun		
Oct				Abdallah al-Qassab	
25 Dec				Umar al-Nazmi	
1944 4 June				Mustafa al-Umari	
July			Riad al-Sulh		
9 Oct	Ahmad Mahir Pasha				
14 Oct		Faris al-Khuri			
1945 10 Jan			Wasi Naim		
25 Feb	Mahmud Fahmy al-Nuqrashi Pasha				

INT (A)

		EGYPT	SYRIA	LEBANON	IRAQ	TRANS-JORDAN
		al-Nuqrashi	al-Khuri	Naim	al-Umari	al-Anabtawi
1945	Mar		Sabri al-Asali			
	19 May					Mushallah al-Attar
	23 Aug			Yusuf Salim		
	27 Aug		Lutfi Haffar			
1946	17 Feb	Ismail Sidqi Pasha				
	23 Feb				Said Salih	
	22 May			Saadi al-Munlah		
	1 June				Abdallah al-Qassab	
	Aug				Arshad al-Umari	
	21 Nov				General Nuri Pasha al-Said	
	10 Dec	Mahmud Fahmy al-Nuqrashi Pasha				
	15 Dec			Sabri Hamadah		Abd al-Mahdi Bey
	28 Dec		Jamil Bey Mardam			
1947	6 Feb					Abbas Mirza Pasha
	30 Mar				Salih Jabir	
	8 June			Camille Chamoun		
	7 Oct		Muhsin al-Barazi			
1948	29 Jan				Jamil al-Midfa'i	
	4 Mar				Nasrat al-Farisi	
	26 June				Mustafa al-Umari	
	26 July			Gabriel Murr		
	23 Aug		Sabri al-Asali			
	Oct				Umar al-Nazmi	
	16 Dec		Adil al-Azmah			

INT (A)

	EGYPT	SYRIA	LEBANON	IRAQ	JORDAN
	al-Nuqrashi	al-Azmah	Murr	al-Nazmi	Mirza
1948 28 Dec	Ibrahim Abd al-Hadi Pasha				
1949 6 Jan				General Nuri Pasha al-Said	
18 Mar				Tawfig al-Naib	
17 Apr		General Husni al-Zaim			
7 May					Said al-Mufti
26 July	Husayn Sirri Pasha				
17 Aug		Rushdi Kikhia			
Sept				Umar al-Nazmi	
1 Oct			Riad al-Sulh		
24 Dec		Ahmad Kanbar			
27 Dec		Samih Qanbar			
1950 12 Jan	Fuad Serag al-Din Pasha				
5 Feb				Salih Jabir	
13 Apr					Falah al-Madadihah
4 June		Rashid Barmada			
16 Sept				General Nuri Pasha al-Said	
14 Oct					Abd al-Rahman Pasha Khalifah
4 Dec					Abbas Pasha Mirza
1951 6 Feb				Umar al-Nazmi	
13 Feb			Husayn al-Uwayni		
27 Mar		Samih Kabbara			
7 June			Abdallah al-Yafi		
25 July					Said al-Mufti

INT (A)

		EGYPT	SYRIA	LEBANON	IRAQ	JORDAN
		al-Din Serag	Kabbara	al-Yafi	al-Nazmi	al-Mufti
1951	9 Aug		Rashid Barmada			
	28 Nov		Ahmad Qanbar			
	3 Dec		*None (Note 21)*			
1952	27 Jan	Murtada al-Maraghi Bey				
	11 Feb			Samih al-Sulh		
	9 June		Colonel Fawzi Silo			
	2 July	Muhammad Hashem Pasha				
	12 July				Mustafa al-Umari	
	22 July	Murtada al-Maraghi Bey				
	24 July	Ali Mahir Pasha				
	7 Sept	Sulayman Hafiz				
	10 Sept			Nazim Akkari		
	18 Sept			General Fuad Shihab		
	1 Oct			Khalid Shihab		
	23 Nov				General Nur al-Din Mahmud	
1953	29 Jan				Hussam al-Din Jumaa	
	12 Apr		Colonel Adib al-Shishakli			
	1 May			Saeb Salem		
	5 May					Bahjat al-Talhouni
	18 June	Colonel Gemal Abd al-Nasr				
	19 July		Nuri Ibesh			
	13 Aug			Abdallah al-Yafi		
	17 Sept				Muhammad Said al-Qazzaz	

INT (A)

	EGYPT	SYRIA	LEBANON	IRAQ	JORDAN
	Abd al-Nassir	Ibesh	al-Yafi	al-Qazzaz	al-Talhouni
1953 4 Oct	Colonel Zakariah Mohieddin				
6 Nov					Haza' al-Majali
1954 26 Jan		Abd al-Rahman al-Hunaydi			
1 Mar		Ali Buzo	Georges Harawi		
4 May					Hashim al-Jayyusi
15 June				Fakhri al-Tabaqgali	
19 June		Ismail Quli			
4 Aug				Muhammad Said al-Qazzaz	
17 Sept			Gabriel Murr		
24 Oct					Riad al-Muflih
3 Nov		Ahmad Qanbar			
1955 13 Feb		Sabri* al-Asali			
30 May					Haza' al-Handawi
9 July			Muhi al-Din Nusuli		
13 Sept		Ali Buzo			
19 Sept			Rashid Karami		
15 Dec					Abbas Mirza
20 Dec					Umar Matar
1956 9 Jan					Samir al-Rifai
20 Mar			Abdallah al-Yafi		
3 Apr					Falah al-Madadihah
22 May					Muhammad Ali al-Ajlani
14 June		Ahmad Qanbar			
1 July					Umar Matar
29 Oct					Abd al-Halim al-Nimr
27 Nov			Samih al-Sulh		

INT (A)

	EGYPT	SYRIA	LEBANON	IRAQ	JORDAN
	Mohieddin	Qanbar	al-Sulh	al-Qazzaz	al-Nimr
1957 2 Jan		Sabri* al-Asali			
15 Apr					Said al-Mufti
25 Apr					Falah al-Madadihah
20 June				General Samih Fattah	
1958 3 Mar				Muhammad Said al-Qazzaz	
6 Mar		Colonel Abd al-Hamid al-Sarraj (Note 46)			
14 July				Colonel Abd al-Salam Muhammad Arif	
24 Sept			Rashid Karami		
30 Sept				Brigadier Ahmad Muhammad Yahya	
14 Oct			Raymond Eddé		
1959 6 May					Wasfi Mirza
7 Oct			Ali Bazzi		
1960 14 May			Edmond Qasbar		
2 Aug			Saeb Salem		
29 Aug					Falah al-Madadihah
1961 19 May			Abdallah Mashnuq		
28 June					Hassan al-Katib
17 Aug	Abbas Radwan (Note 47)	Colonel Abd al-Hamid al-Sarraj (Note 47)			
30 Sept		Adnan al-Quwatli			
18 Oct	Zakariah Mohieddin				
31 Oct			Kamal Jumblatt		
20 Nov		Abd al-Salam al-Tarmani			
22 Dec		Ahmad Qanbar			

INT (A)

	EGYPT	SYRIA	LEBANON	IRAQ	JORDAN
	Mohieddin	Qanbar	Jumblatt	Yahya	al-Katib
1962 17 Jan					Kamal al-Din Dajani
16 Apr		Abd al-Halim Khaddur			
20 June		General Aziz Abd al-Karim			
29 Sept	Abd al-Aziz Fahmi				
1963 8 Feb				Ali Salih al-Sa'di	
9 Mar		Colonel Amin al-Hafiz			
27 Mar					Salih al-Majali
13 May				Hazim* Jawad	
5 Aug		Nur al-Din al-Atasi			
20 Nov				Rashid Muslih	
1964 20 Feb			Husayn al-Uwayni		
13 May		Fahmi al-Ashuri			
7 July					Muhammad Nazzal al-Arnuti
4 Oct		Colonel* Abd al-Karim al-Jundi			
14 Nov				Colonel Subhi Abd al-Hamid	
18 Nov			Taqi al-Din al-Sulh		
1965 13 Feb					Abd al-Wahhab al-Majali
11 July				General Abd al-Latif al-Darraji	
25 July			Muhammad Knei'o		
23 Sept		Muhammad Id Ashawi			
30 Sept	Zakariah Mohieddin				
1966 1 Jan		Fahmy al-Ashuri			
1 Mar		Muhammad Id Ashawi			

INT (A)

	EGYPT	SYRIA	LEBANON	IRAQ	JORDAN
	Mohieddin	Ashawi	Knei'o	al-Darraji	al-Majali
1966 9 Apr			Pierre Gemayel		
18 Apr				Abd al-Rahman al-Bazzaz	
9 Aug				Brigadier Rajab Abd al-Majid	
10 Sept	Sharawi Muhammad Gomaa				
7 Dec			Badri al-Meouchi		
22 Dec					Wasfi Mirza
1967 23 Apr					General Radi Abdallah
10 May				Brigadier Abd al-Sattar Abd al-Latif	
10 July				General Tahir Yahya	
20 Aug				Dr Shamil Samarrai	
7 Oct					Hassan Kayid
1968 8 Feb			Sulayman Franjiyeh		
25 Apr					Bahjat al-Talhouni
3 July			Abdallah al-Yafi		
17 July				General Salih Mahdi Ammash	
9 Sept					Dayfullah al-Hamud
20 Oct			Pierre Gemayel		
29 Oct		Colonel Muhammad Rabah Tawil			
26 Dec					Musa Abu Raghib
1969 15 Jan			Adil Usayran		
24 Mar					Aqif al-Fayiz
30 June					General Muhammad Rassoul Kilani

75

INT (A)

	EGYPT	SYRIA	LEBANON	IRAQ	JORDAN
	Gomaa	Tawil	Usayran	Ammash	Kilani
1969 25 Nov			Kamal Jumblatt		
1970 23 Feb					Musa* Abu Raghib
3 Apr				General Sa'dun Ghaidan	
19 Apr					Najib Irshidat
27 June					Sulayman al-Hadidi
16 Sept					Brigadier Salih Shara
13 Oct			Saeb Salem		
28 Oct					Brigadier Mazin Ajlouni
21 Nov		Brigadier Abd al-Rahman Khulaifawi			
1971 3 Apr		Brigadier Ali Zaza			
14 May	Memduh Salim				
22 May					Ibrahim al-Habashinah
1972 21 Aug					Ahmad al-Tarawnah

MINISTERS OF THE INTERIOR INT (B)

	MOROCCO	ALGERIA	TUNISIA	LIBYA	SUDAN	SOUTHERN YEMEN
1954 9 Jan					Ismail al-Azhari	
1955 17 Sept			Mongi Slim			
7 Dec	Qaid Lahcen Lyoussi					
1956 14 Apr			Tayeb Mehiri			
4 May	Driss Mhammedi					
7 July					Ali Abd al-Rahman	
1958 26 Mar					Mirghani Hamza	
8 May	Mas'ud Chiguer					
19 Sept		Lakhdar ben Tobal (Note 30)				
18 Nov					General Ahmad Abd al-Wahhab	
24 Dec	Driss Mhammedi					
1959 9 Mar					Brigadier Ahmad Mahgoub Buhri	
1960 26 May	M'barek Bekkai					
1961 2 Feb					Brigadier Maqbul al-Amin	
14 Apr	Ahmad Reda Guedira					
27 Aug		Krim Belkacem (Note 30)				
1962 28 Sept		Ahmad Madaghri				
15 Dec				Ahmad Awn Suf		
20 Dec					Muhammad Ahmad Urwah	
1963 6 Mar				Wanis al-Qadafi		
5 June	Ahmad Hamyani					
13 Nov	Abd al-Rahman Khatib					
1964 22 Jan				Mahmud Muntasir		
26 Mar				Umar al-Baruni		

77

INT (B)

	MOROCCO	ALGERIA	TUNISIA	LIBYA	SUDAN	SOUTHERN YEMEN
	Khatib	Madaghri	Mehiri	al-Baruni	Urwah	
1964 30 May				Mahmud al-Bishti		
20 July		Ahmad ben Bella				
20 Aug	General Muhammad Oufkir					
29 Oct				Fadhl al-Amir		
30 Oct					Clement Mboro	
1965 17 June					Ahmad al-Mahdi	
6 July			Qaid Beji Essibsi			
10 July		Ahmad Madaghri				
2 Oct				Ahmad Awn Suf		
1966 4 Aug					Abdallah Abd al-Rahman Nagdallah	
1967 4 Apr				Ali as-Sahili		
27 May					Hassan Awadhallah	
1 July				Ahmad Awn Suf		
1 Dec						Muhammad Ali Haitham
1969 26 May					Major Faruq Hamadallah	
9 June				Matuq Adam		
23 June						Muhammad Salah Yafai
8 Sept			Muhammad Hadi Kefacha	Colonel Musa Ahmad		
10 Dec				Colonel Muammar al-Qadafi		
1970 16 Jan				Major Abd al-Salam Jaloud		
12 June			Ahmad Mestiri			
16 Sept				Captain Abd al-Moneim Tahir Houni		

INT (B)

78

INT (B)

	MOROCCO	ALGERIA	TUNISIA	LIBYA	SUDAN	SOUTHERN YEMEN
	Oufkir	Madaghri	Mestiri	Houni	Hamadallah	Yafai
1970 17 Oct				Major Khuwaildi Hamidi		
16 Nov					Major Abu al-Qasim Ibrahim	
1971 2 Aug						Muhammad Salah Muti
6 Aug	Ahmad ben Boushta					
13 Aug				Major Abd al-Moneim Tahir Houni		
4 Sept			Hedi Nouira			
14 Oct					General Muhammad al-Baqr Ahmad	
29 Oct			Muhammad Hadi Kefacha			
1972 12 Apr	Dr Mohammed Benhima					
2 Nov				Major Khuwaildi Hamidi		

INT (C) MINISTERS OF THE INTERIOR

		SAUDI ARABIA	YEMEN	KUWAIT	BAHRAIN	QATAR	OMAN	UNION OF ARAB EMIRATES
1953	9 Oct	Prince Abdallah al-Faysal (Note 31)						
1955	31 Aug		Ahmad Muhammad al-Siyaghi (Note 32)					
1960	21 Dec	Prince Abd al-Muhsin ben Abd al-Aziz						
1961	11 Sept	Prince Faysal ben Turki						
1962	17 Jan			Shaykh Sa'd al-Abdallah				
	28 Sept		Abd al-Latif Dayfallah					
	31 Oct	Prince Fahad ben Abd al-Aziz						
1963	25 Apr		Muhammad al-Ra'ini					
1965	6 Jan		Abdallah Husayn ben al-Ahmad					
	20 July		Qadi Muhammad al-Zuhayr					
1966	13 Apr		Brigadier Husayn al-Daf'i					
	18 Sept		Brigadier Muhammad al-Ahnumi					
1967	12 Oct		Colonel Abdallah al-Dhabbi					
	5 Nov		Abd al-Salam Sabra					
	21 Dec		Colonel Abdallah Barakat					
1968	15 Sept		Abd al-Salam Sabra (Note 48)					
1970	8 Aug		Colonel Abdallah al-Dhabbi					
	15 Aug						Shaykh Badr ben Saud (Note 49)	
1971	3 May		Abd al-Salam Sabra (Note 50)					

INT (C)

		SAUDI ARABIA	YEMEN	KUWAIT	BAHRAIN	QATAR	OMAN	UNION OF ARAB EMIRATES
1971	18 Sept	Fahad	Sabra Colonel Ibrahim al-Hamidi *(Note 51)*	Sa'd al-Abdallah		Badr ben Saud		
	9 Dec							Shaykh Mubarak Muhammad al-Nahayan
1972	2 Jan						Sultan ben Hammoud	
	18 June					Shaykh Khalid ben Hamad		
	30 Dec		Brigadier Muhammad Ali al-Ashwal					

MINISTERS OF FINANCE

FIN (A)

	EGYPT	SYRIA	LEBANON	IRAQ	TRANS-JORDAN
1900 1 Jan	Mazloum Pasha				
1908 12 Nov	Ahmad Hishmet Pasha				
1910 22 Feb	Sir Joseph Saba Pasha				
1912 15 Apr	Ahmad Hilmi Pasha				
1914 5 Apr	Yusuf Wahba Pasha				
1919 Mar	*None*				
9 Apr	Yusuf Wahba Pasha				
23 Apr	*None*				
21 May	Yusuf Wahba Pasha				
1920 8 Mar		Faris al-Khuri			
20 May	Mahmud Fakhry Pasha				
25 July		*None (Note 1)*			
11 Nov				Sassoon Effendi Haskail *(Note 19)*	
1921 16 Mar	Ismail Sidqi Pasha				
1922 30 Nov	Yusuf Sulayman Pasha				
1923 15 Mar	Muhammad Muhib Pasha				
6 Aug	Ahmad Hishmet Pasha				
22 Nov				Muhsin al-Shallash	
1924 28 Jan	Muhammad Tawfiq Nasim Pasha				
2 Aug				Sassoon Effendi Haskail	
18 Nov	Ali Bey al-Shamsi				

83

FIN (A)

	EGYPT	SYRIA	LEBANON	IRAQ	TRANS-JORDAN
	al-Shamsi	*None*		Haskail	
1924 24 Nov	Yusuf Qattawi Pasha				
1925 Jan		Jalal Bey Zuhdi			
13 Mar	Yahya Ibrahim Pasha				
26 June				Raouf Bey al-Jadbirgi	
21 Dec		*None (Note 2)*			
1926 4 May		Shakir Bey Nimah			
31 May			Auguste Adib Pasha		
7 June	Morqos Hanna Pasha				
12 June		Abd al-Qadir Bey al-Azm			
21 Nov				General Yasin Pasha al-Hashimi	
6 Dec		Hamdi Bey al-Nasr			
1927 26 Apr	Muhammad Mahmud Pasha				
5 May			Amir Khalid Shihab		
1928 5 Jan			Husayn Bey Ahdab		
11 Jan				Yusuf Effendi Ghanimah	
15 Feb		Jamil Bey al-Ulshi			
27 June	Ali Mahir Pasha				
10 Aug			Subhi Bey Haydar		
1929 9 May			Husayn Bey Ahdab		

FIN (A)

	EGYPT	SYRIA	LEBANON	IRAQ	TRANS-JORDAN
	Mahir	al-Ulshi	Ahdab	Ghanimah	
1929 19 Sept				General Yasin Pasha al-Hashimi	
4 Oct	Mustafa Mahir Pasha				
8 Oct					Awda Bey al-Qasus
11 Oct			Musa Nammur		
1930 1 Jan	William Makram Obeid Pasha				
23 Mar				Ali Jawdat	
25 Mar			Auguste Adib Pasha		
10 June		Tawfiq al-Shamiya			
20 June	Ismail Sidqi Pasha				
Sept				Jamil al-Midfa'i	
2 Nov				Rustem Bey Haydar	
1931 21 Feb					Shukri Bey Sha'sha'ah
Nov		*None (Note 2)*			
1932 May			*None (Note 2)*		
7 June		Jamil Bey Mardam			
3 Nov				Nasrat Bey al-Farisi	
1933 20 Mar				General Yasin Pasha al-Hashimi	
5 May		Shakir Bey Nimat al-Shibani			
21 Sept	Hassan Sabri Bey				
9 Nov				Nasrat Bey al-Farisi	

FIN (A)

	EGYPT	SYRIA	LEBANON	IRAQ	TRANS-JORDAN
	Sabri	al-Shibani	*None*	al-Farisi	Sha'sha'ah
1934 21 Feb				Naji Pasha al-Suwaydi	
16 Mar		Henry Hindiyyeh			
27 Aug				Yusuf Bey Ghanimah	
15 Nov	Ahmad Abd al-Wahhab Pasha				
1935 17 Mar				General Yasin Pasha al-Hashimi	
25 Mar				Rauf Bey al-Bahrani	
1936 22 Feb		Edmond Homsi			
9 May	William Makram Obeid Pasha				
30 Oct				Ja'far Abu al-Timam	
21 Dec		Shukri Bey al-Quwatli			
1937 5 Jan			Amir Khalid Abu al-Lam		
13 Mar			Khair al-Din al-Ahdab		
24 June				Muhammad Ali Mahmud	
10 July			Georges Thabit		
17 Aug				Ibrahim Kamal	
31 Oct			Musa Nammur		
29 Dec	Ismail Sidqi Pasha				
1938 18 Mar			Camille Chamoun		
21 Mar		Jamil Bey Mardam			
18 May	Muhammad Mahmud Pasha				
24 June	Dr Ahmad Mahir				

FIN (A)

	EGYPT	SYRIA	LEBANON	IRAQ	TRANS-JORDAN
	Mahir	Mardam	Chamoun	Kamal	Sha'sha'ah
1938 27 July		Lutfi al-Haffar			
24 Oct			Hamid Franjiyeh		
25 Dec				Rustem Bey Haydar	
1939 22 Jan			Musa Nammur		
23 Feb		Fa'iz al-Khuri			
6 Apr		Muhammad Khalil al-Mudarris			
10 July		Husni al-Baytar			
6 Aug					Abdallah Bey al-Nimr
18 Aug	Husayn Sirri Pasha				
21 Sept			*None (Note 22)*		
1940 20 Feb				Raouf Bey al-Bahrani	
6 Mar					Nicola Bey Ghanimah
1 Apr				Naji Bey al-Suwaydi	
28 June	Abd al-Hamid Sulayman Pasha				
2 Sept	Mahmud Fahmy al-Nuqrashi Pasha				
23 Sept	Abd al-Hamid Sulayman Pasha				
15 Nov	Hassan Sadiq Pasha				
5 Dec	Abd al-Hamid Badawi Pasha				
1941 3 Feb				Ali Mumtaz	
4 Apr		Hanin Sahnawi			
7 Apr			Joseph Najjar		

FIN (A)

	EGYPT	SYRIA	LEBANON	IRAQ	TRANS-JORDAN
	Badawi	Sahnawi	Najjar	Mumtaz	Ghanimah
1941 13 Apr				Naji Bey al-Suwaydi	
4 June				Ibrahim Kamal	
21 Sept		Hassan al-Hakim			
11 Oct				Ali Mumtaz	
1 Dec			Ahmad al-Da'uq		
1942 6 Feb	William Makram Obeid Pasha				
19 Apr		Fa'iz al-Khuri			
26 May	Kamal Sidqi Pasha				
July			Musa Nammur		
9 Oct				Salih Jabir	
1943 10 Jan		Amir Mustafa al-Shihabi			
22 Mar			Amir Khalid Shihab		
1 June	Sir Amin Osman Pasha				
24 June				Jalal Baban	
1 Aug			Abdallah Bayhum		
25 Sept			Riad al-Sulh		
Oct				Abd al-Illah al-Hafiz	
25 Dec				Ali Mumtaz	
1944 4 June				Salih Jabir	
July			Hamid Franjiyeh		
9 Oct	William Makram Obeid Pasha				
14 Oct		Khalid Pasha al-Azm			
1945 10 Jan			Abd al-Hamid Karami		

FIN (A)

FIN (A)

	EGYPT	SYRIA	LEBANON	IRAQ	TRANS-JORDAN
	Obeid	al-Azm	Karami	Jabir	Ghanimah
1945 9 Apr		Naim Bey al-Antaki			
19 May					Said Pasha al-Mufti
23 Aug			Emile Lahud		
27 Aug		Khalid Pasha al-Azm			
1 Oct		Naim Bey al-Antaki			
1946 23 Feb				Abd al-Wahhab Mahmud	
17 Feb	Ismail Sidqi Pasha				
22 May			Camille Chamoun		
1 June				Yusuf Ghanimah	
30 June	Abd al-Rahman al-Biyali				
21 Nov				Salih Jabir	
10 Dec	Ibrahim Abd al-Hadi Pasha				
28 Dec		Said al-Ghazzi			
1947 19 Jan				Abd al-Illah al-Hafiz	
6 Feb					Sulayman Bey Nabulsi
18 Feb	Abd al-Majid Badr Pasha				
29 Mar				Yusuf Ghanimah	
8 June			Muhammad al-Abbud		
7 Oct		Wahbi Hariri			
19 Nov	Mahmud Fahmy al-Nuqrashi Pasha				
1948 29 Jan				Sadiq al-Bassam	
26 June				Ali Mumtaz	
26 July			Husayn al-Uwayni		

FIN (A)

	EGYPT	SYRIA	LEBANON	IRAQ	JORDAN
	al-Nuqrashi	Hariri	al-Uwayni	Mumtaz	Nabulsi
1948 Nov				Khalil Ismail	
17 Dec		Hassan Jabbarah			
28 Dec	Ibrahim Abd al-Hadi Pasha				
1949 15 Jan	Husayn Fahmy Bey				
7 May					Sulayman al-Sukkar
17 Aug		Khalid Pasha al-Azm			
3 Nov	Abd al-Shafi' Abd al-Mutaal Bey				
10 Dec				Ali Mumtaz	
24 Dec		Shakir al-As			
28 Dec		Abd al-Rahman al-Azm			
1950 12 Jan	Dr Muhammad Zaki Abd al-Mutaal Bey				
5 Feb				Abd al-Karim al-Uzri	
4 June		Hassan Jabbarah			
8 Sept		Shakir al-As			
16 Sept				Abd al-Wahhab Mirjan	
11 Nov	Fuad Serag al-Din Pasha				
4 Dec					Sulayman Pasha al-Nabulsi
1951 13 Feb			Boulos Fayad		
27 Mar		Abd al-Rahman al-Azm			
7 June			Philippe Taqla		
25 July					Salah Pasha Khalifa
9 Aug		Hassan al-Hakim			
8 Sept					Abd al-Halim Hamud

FIN (A)

	EGYPT	SYRIA	LEBANON	IRAQ	JORDAN
	Serag al-Din	al-Hakim	Taqla	Mirjan	Hamud
1951 28 Nov		Abd al-Rahman al-Azm			
3 Dec		*None* (Note 21)			
1952 27 Jan	Dr Muhammad Zaki Abd al-Mutaal				
11 Feb			Emile Lahud		
9 June		Said al-Zaim			
2 July	*Neguib Ibrahim Pasha				
12 July				Ibrahim al-Shahbandar	
22 July	Dr Muhammad Zaki Abd al-Mutaal				
24 July	Abd al-Jalil al-Imari				
10 Sept			Basil Trad		
30 Sept					Musa Nasr
1 Oct			Georges Hakim		
23 Nov				Ali Mahmud al-Shaikli	
1953 29 Jan				Ali Mumtaz	
1 May			Georges Karam		
5 May					Sulayman al-Sukkar
19 July		Georges Shahin			
13 Aug			Pierre Eddé		
17 Sept				Abd al-Karim al-Uzri	
1954 26 Feb	Dr Ali al-Garaitli				
1 Mar		Abd al-Rahman-al-Azm	Abdallah al-Yafi		
8 Mar				Ali Mumtaz	
18 Mar	Abd al-Jalil al-Imari				
18 Apr	Abd al-Hamid al-Sharif				
29 Apr				Abd al-Majid Mahmud	

FIN (A)

	EGYPT	SYRIA	LEBANON	IRAQ	JORDAN
	al-Sharif	al-Azm	al-Yafi	Mahmud	al-Sukkar
1954 4 May					Abd al-Rahman Khalifah
19 June		Izzat Sakkal			
4 Aug				Dr Dhia Ja'far	
1 Sept	Dr Abd al-Moneim al-Qaysuni				
17 Sept			Muhi al-Din Nusuli		
24 Oct					Anastas Hananiyah
3 Nov		Rizqallah al-Antaki			
1955 13 Feb		Leon Zamarya			
30 May					Bishara Ghusayb
9 July			Pierre Eddé		
13 Sept		Abd al-Wahhab Humad			
19 Sept			Jamil Shihab		
17 Dec				Khalil Kunnah	
20 Dec					Khulusi al-Khayri
1956 9 Jan					Hashim al-Jayyusi
20 Mar			Georges Karam		
22 May					Bishara Ghusayb
14 June		Sabri al-Asali			
29 Oct					Salah Tuqan
19 Nov			Nasri Maalouf		
1957 2 Jan		Asad Mahasan			
15 Apr					Sulayman al-Sukkar
25 Apr					Anastas Hananiyah
20 June				Ali Mumtaz	
26 June		Sabri* al-Asali			
18 Aug			Jamil Makkawi		
17 Nov		Khalid Pasha al-Azm			

FIN (A)

	EGYPT	SYRIA	LEBANON	IRAQ	JORDAN
	al-Qaysuni	al-Azm	Makkawi	Mumtaz	Hananiyah
1957 15 Dec				Dr Nadim al-Pachachi	
1958 3 Feb			Farid Quzma		
3 Mar				Abd al-Karim al-Uzri (Note 52)	
6 Mar		(Note 53)			
14 Mar			Pierre Eddé		
9 July					Ahmad al-Tarawnah
14 July				Muhammad Hadid	
1 Aug			Joseph Shader		
24 Sept			Rafiq Naja		
14 Oct			Rashid Karami		
1959 27 Jan					Saman Daud
6 May					Hashim al-Jayyusi
1960 26 Apr				Abd al-Latif al-Shawaf	
14 May			Amin Bayhum		
2 Aug			Pierre Gemayel		
15 Nov				Dr Muzaffar Husayn Jamil	
1961 30 Sept		Leon Zamarya			
31 Oct			Rashid Karami		
20 Nov		Numan al-Azhari			
22 Dec		Rashid al-Daqr			
1962 16 Apr		Georges Khuri			
17 Sept		Khalil Kallas			
1963 27 Jan					Izz al-Din al-Mufti
8 Feb				Salih Kubbah	
15 Feb		Izzat al-Tarabulsi			
9 Mar		Abd al-Wahhab Humad			
27 Mar					Abd al-Rahman Khalifah

FIN (A)

	EGYPT	SYRIA	LEBANON	IRAQ	JORDAN
	al-Qaysuni	Humad	Karami	Kubbah	Khalifah
1963 21 Apr					Abd al-Latif Anabtawi
13 May		Mustafa al-Shamma		Muhammad Jawad al-Ubusi	
10 July					Abd al-Rahman Khalifah
7 Oct				Salman Abd al-Razzaq al-Aswad	
20 Nov				Muhammad Jawad al-Ubusi	
30 Nov					Nizam al-Sharabi
1964 20 Feb			Amin Bayhum		
7 July					Hashim al-Jayyusi
4 Oct		Abd al-Fattah al-Bushi			
18 Nov			Uthman al-Dana		
1965 13 Feb					Izz al-Din al-Mufti
25 July			Rashid Karami		
11 Aug				Abd al-Hasan Zalzalah	
6 Sept				Salman Abd al-Razzaq al-Aswad	
21 Sept				Shukri Salah Zaki	
2 Oct	Labib Shuqayr *(Note 54)*				
1966 1 Jan		Muwaffaq al-Sharbaji			
9 Apr			Abdallah al-Yafi		
9 Aug				Dr Abdallah al-Naqshabandi	
10 Sept	Hassan Zaki				
17 Oct				Dr Khalid al-Shawi	
7 Dec			Rashid Karami		
22 Dec					Said Dajani
1967 23 Apr					Abd al-Wahhab al-Majali
10 May				Abd al-Rahman al-Habib	

FIN (A)

		EGYPT	SYRIA	LEBANON	IRAQ	JORDAN
		Zaki	al-Sharbaji	Karami	al-Habib	al-Majali
1967	7 Oct					Hashim al-Jayyusi
1968	8 Feb			Abdallah al-Yafi		
	3 July			Pierre Eddé		
	17 July				Salih Kubbah	
	31 July				Amin Abd al-Karim	
	12 Oct			Pierre Gemayel		
	20 Oct			Abdallah al-Yafi		
1969	15 Jan			Pierre Gemayel		
	23 Jan			Rashid Karami		
	24 Mar					Fadil al-Dalqamouni
	29 May		Dr Nourallah Nourallah			
	12 Aug					Yakoub Muammar
1970	19 Apr					Dr Wasfi Anabtawi
	27 June					Abd al-Qadir Tash
	16 Sept					Brigadier Fahad Jaradat
	26 Sept					Fawwaz Rousan
	13 Oct			Elias Saba		
	28 Oct					Ahmad Lawzi
	18 Nov	Muhammad Marziban				
1971	29 Nov					Anis al-Muashir
1972	27 May			Fuad Naffaa		
	21 Aug					Farid al-Sa'd

FIN (B) — MINISTERS OF FINANCE

	MOROCCO	ALGERIA	TUNISIA	LIBYA	SUDAN	SOUTHERN YEMEN
1951 29 Mar				Mansur ben Qadara		
1953 20 Sept				Dr Ali al-Unayzi		
1954 9 Jan					Hamad Tawfiq	
1955 17 Sept			Hedi Nouira			
7 Dec	Abd al-Qadir Benjelloun					
1956 2 Feb					Ibrahim Ahmad	
26 Mar				Ismail ben al-Amin		
26 Oct	Abd al-Rahim Bouabid					
1958 27 Apr				Miftah Uraiqib		
19 Sept		Ahmad Francis (Note 30)				
14 Oct				Ismail Ben al-Amin		
18 Nov					Abd al-Majid Ahmad	
30 Dec			Ahmad Mestiri			
1960 26 May	Muhammad Douiri					
27 Sept				Muhammad ben Othman		
17 Oct				Salim Lutfi al-Qadi		
1961 3 Jan			Ahmad Ben Salah			
4 May				Ahmad al-Hasairi		
27 Aug		Yusuf ben Khedda (Note 30)				
1962 28 Sept		Ahmad Francis				
11 Oct				Muhammad Sulayman Burbidah		
1963 4 Jan	Driss Slaoui					
19 Mar				Mansur ben Qadara		
5 Sept		Bashir Boumaza				
16 Nov					Ma'mun Bihayri	
1964 22 Jan				Salim Lutfi al-Qadi		

FIN (B)

	MOROCCO	ALGERIA	TUNISIA	LIBYA	SUDAN	SOUTHERN YEMEN
	Slaoui	Boumaza	ben Salah	al-Qadi	Bihayri	
1964 20 Aug	Muhammad Cherkaoui					
30 Oct					Mubarak Zarrouk	
15 Nov				Umar al-Baruni		
1965 8 June	Mamoun Tahiri					
17 June					Ibrahim al-Mufti	
10 July		Ahmad Kaid				
19 July					Husayn al-Hindi	
2 Oct				Salim Lutfi al-Qadi		
1966 4 Aug					Hamza Mirghani	
1967 27 May					Husayn al-Hindi	
1 Dec						Mahmud Abdallah Ushaysh
15 Dec		Ahmad* Madaghri				
1968 4 Jan				Abd al-Hadi al-Qaoud		
7 Mar		Cherif Belkacem				
1969 12 Feb						Sayf Ahmad al-Dhalai
25 May					Mansur Mahgoub	
23 June						Mahmud Abdallah Ushaysh
8 Sept			Abd al-Razzaq Rasaa			
8 Sept				Mahmud al-Maghribi		
1970 17 Jan				Muhammad Hilal Rabi		
17 Mar		Ahmad Madaghri				
26 Mar	Abd al-Karim Lazraq					
29 June						Mahfouz Bashwan
22 July		Ismail Mahroug				

FIN (B)

	MOROCCO	ALGERIA	TUNISIA	LIBYA	SUDAN	SOUTHERN YEMEN
	Lazraq	Mahroug	Rasaa	Rabi	Mahgoub	Bashwan
1970 16 Sept				Captain Umar Abdallah Muhaishi		
17 Oct				Major Abd al-Salam Jaloud		
1971 12 Feb					Brigadier Muhammad Muhammad Abd al-Halim	
23 Apr	Karim Lamrani					
2 Aug						Mahmud Abdallah Ushaysh
29 Oct			Muhammad Fitouri			
1972 22 Jan						Fadhl Muhsin Abdallah
8 Apr					Musa al-Mubarak	
12 Apr	Mustafa Faris					
16 July				Muhammad Zarouk Rajab		
9 Oct					Ibrahim Ilyas	
19 Nov	Bensalem Guessous					

MINISTERS OF FINANCE

FIN (C)

		SAUDI ARABIA	YEMEN	KUWAIT	BAHRAIN	QATAR	OMAN	UNION OF ARAB EMIRATES
1953	9 Oct	Abdallah Sulayman ben Hamdan *(Note 55)*						
1954	30 Aug	Muhammad Sarur al-Sabban						
1955	31 Aug		Abd al-Rahman al-Siyaghi *(Note 56)*					
1957			Muhammad Ahmad al-Hajari					
1958	28 July	Crown Prince Faysal ben Abd al-Aziz *(Note 57)*						
1960	Aug		Muhammad Uthman					
	21 Dec	Prince Talal ben Abd al-Aziz						
1961	11 Sept	Prince Muhammad ben Saud						
	16 Sept	Prince Nawaf ben Abd al-Aziz						
1962	17 Jan			Shaykh Jabir al-Ahmad				
	15 Mar	Prince Musa'id ben Abd al-Rahman						
	31 Oct		Abd al-Ghani Ali Ahmad *(Note 58)*					
1965	24 Apr		Ahmad Abduh *(Note 59)*					
	20 July		Ahmad al-Rahumi *(Note 60)*					
	4 Dec			Shaykh Sabah al-Ahmad *(Note 61)*				
1966	18 Sept		Abd al-Ghani Ali Ahmad *(Note 62)*					
1967	4 Feb			Abd al-Rahman Salim al-Atiki				
	5 Nov		Ahmad Abdu Said *(Note 63)*					

FIN (C)

	SAUDI ARABIA	YEMEN	KUWAIT	BAHRAIN	QATAR	OMAN	UNION OF ARAB EMIRATES
	Musa'id	Said	al-Atiki				
1968 15 Sept		Ahmad al-Rahumi *(Note 64)*					
1969 3 Apr		Muhammad ben Ismail al-Rabi *(Note 65)*					
2 Sept		Ali Lutfi al-Nur *(Note 66)*					
1970 19 Jan				Mahmud al-Alawi			
5 Feb		Abd al-Karim al-Ansi *(Note 67)*					
29 May					Shaykh Khalifa ben Hamad *(Note 68)*		
1971 1 Mar						Saiyyid Faysal ben Ali	
3 May		Muhammad ben Ismail al-Rabi *(Note 69)*					
8 Aug						Abd al-Hafiz Salim Rajab	
24 Aug		Dr Muhammad Said al-Attar *(Note 70)*					
18 Sept		Abdallah Abd al-Majid al-Asnag *(Note 71)*					
9 Dec							Shaykh Hamdan ben Rashid al-Maktum
1972 11 Dec					Shaykh Abdul Aziz ben Khalifa		

MINISTERS OF OIL

		IRAQ	SAUDI ARABIA	LIBYA	KUWAIT	SYRIA	QATAR	EGYPT
1959	July	Ibrahim Kubbah						
1960	16 Feb	Brigadier* Ahmad Yahya Ibrahim						
	9 Dec	Muhammad Salman						
	21 Dec		Abdallah al-Tariki					
1961	4 May			Fuad Kabazi				
1962	28 Jan			Nuri ben Gharsah				
	15 Mar		Ahmad Zaki Yamani					
	11 Oct			Wahbi al-Buri				
1963	8 Feb	Abd al-Aziz al-Wattari						
	13 Nov			Ali Nur al-Din al-Unayzi				
1964	25 Mar							Dr Aziz Sidqi
	26 Mar			Fuad Kabazi				
1965	6 Sept	Abd al-Rahman al-Bazzaz						
	21 Sept	Shukri Salih Zaki						
	1 Oct							Dr Mustafa Khalil
	4 Dec				Shaykh Sabah al-Ahmad (Note 61)			
1966	9 Aug	General Naji Talib						
	10 Sept							Dr Mahmud Yunis
	16 Oct					Dr Asad Taqla		
1967	4 Feb				Abd al-Rahman Salim al-Atiki			
	4 Apr			Khalifa Musa				
	10 May	Abd al-Sattar Husayn						
	28 Sept					Dr Ahmad Hassan		
1968	20 Mar							Dr Aziz Sidqi

OIL

OIL

	IRAQ	SAUDI ARABIA	LIBYA	KUWAIT	SYRIA	QATAR	EGYPT
	Husayn	Yamani	Musa	al-Atiki	Hassan		Sidqi
1968 20 July	Dr Mahdi Hantoush						
31 July	Dr Rashid al-Rifa'						
1969 8 Sept			Anis Shtaiwi				
31 Dec	Dr Sa'dun Hammadi						
1970 16 Jan			Izz al-Din Mabrouk				
29 May						Shaykh Khalifa ben Hamad *(Note 68)*	
21 Nov					Dr Mustafa Haddad		
1972 17 Jan							Dr Yahya al-Mullah
23 Mar					Ahmad Abbara		
11 Dec						Shaykh Abdul Aziz ben Khalifa	
24 Dec					Fayiz al-Nasir		

BRITISH/FRENCH REPRESENTATIVES

REP (A)

		EGYPT (Note 72)	SYRIA-LEBANON (Note 73)	IRAQ (Note 74)	TRANS-JORDAN (Note 75)
1900	1 Jan	Lord Cromer			
1907	7 May	Sir Eldon Gorst			
1911	6 Sept	Field Marshal Earl Kitchener of Khartoum			
1914	Nov			Sir Percy Cox	
	18 Dec	Sir Henry McMahon			
1917	1 Jan	Sir Reginald Wingate			
	9 Apr		François Georges-Picot		
1918	28 May			Colonel Arnold Wilson	
1919	14 Oct	Field Marshal Lord Allenby			
	21 Nov		General Joseph Gouraud		
1920	1 July				Sir Herbert Samuel
	3 Oct			Sir Percy Cox	
1923	Apr		General Maxime Weygand		
1924	4 May			Sir Henry Dobbs	
1925	2 Jan		General Maurice Sarrail		
	25 Aug				Field Marshal Lord Plumer
	12 Oct	Lord Lloyd			
	6 Nov		Henri de Jouvenel		
1926	27 Aug		Henri Ponsot		
1928	6 Dec				Sir John Chancellor
1929	3 Mar			Sir Gilbert Clayton	
	27 Aug	Sir Percy Loraine			
	3 Oct			Sir Francis Humphrys	

103

REP (A)

	EGYPT	SYRIA-LEBANON	IRAQ	TRANS-JORDAN
	Loraine	Ponsot	Humphrys	Chancellor
1931 20 Nov				General Sir Arthur Wauchope
1933 12 Oct		Count Damien de Martel		
16 Dec	Sir Miles Lampson (later Lord Killearn)			
1935 18 Mar			Sir Archibald Clark Kerr	
1938 3 Mar				Sir Harold MacMichael
9 Mar			Sir Maurice Drummond Peterson	
23 Oct		Gabriel Puaux		
1939 3 May			Sir Basil Newton	
1940 9 Dec		General Henri Dentz		
1941 26 Feb			Sir Kinahan Cornwallis	
June		General Georges Catroux		
1943 3 June		Jean Helleu		
1944 Feb		General Paul-Etienne Beynet		
19 July				Field Marshal Lord Gort
1945 28 Mar			Sir Francis Stonehewer-Bird	
8 Nov				General Sir Alan Cunningham
1946 12 Mar	********			
6 July		********		
1948 28 Mar			********	
14 May				********

BRITISH/FRENCH/ITALIAN REPRESENTATIVES

REP (B)

	MOROCCO (Note 76)	ALGERIA (Note 77)	TUNISIA (Note 78)	TRIPO- LITANIA	CYRENAICA	SUDAN	SOUTH ARABIA
1900 1 Jan		Jullien Laferrière	René Millet			Colonel Sir Reginald Wingate	
3 Oct		Charles Célestin Jonnart					
Nov			*Benoit de Merkel				
1901 18 June		Paul Révoil					
27 Dec			Stephen Pichon				
1903 May		Charles Célestin Jonnart					
1906 29 Dec			Gabriel Alapetite				
1911 22 Mar		Charles Lutaud					
1912 28 Apr	General Hubert Lyautey						
1913 2 June				General Vincenzo Garioni			
Oct				General Giovanni Ameglio	General Giovanni Ameglio		
1916 1 Jan						General Sir Lee Stack	
13 Dec	General* Joseph Gouraud						
1917 7 Apr	General Hubert Lyautey						
1918 29 Jan		Charles Célestin Jonnart					
5 Aug				General Vincenzo Garioni	General Vincenzo Garioni		
26 Oct			Etienne Flandin				
1919 1 Aug				Vittorio Menzinger	Giacomo de Martino		
29 Aug		Jean-Baptiste Abel					
1920 6 July				Luigi Mercatelli			
23 Nov			Lucien Saint				
1921 July				Giuseppe Volpi			
29 Aug		Théodore Steeg					

105

REP (B)

	MOROCCO	ALGERIA	TUNISIA	TRIPOLI-TANIA	CYRENAICA	SUDAN	SOUTH ARABIA
	Lyautey	Steeg	Saint	Volpi	de Martino	Stack	
1921 23 Nov					Luigi Pintor		
1923 7 Jan					General Luigi Bongiovanni		
1924 4 May					General Ernesto Mombelli		
4 Dec						Sir Geoffrey Archer	
1925 12 May		Maurice Viollette					
July				General Emilio de Bono			
4 Oct	Théodore Steeg						
1926 24 Oct						Sir John Maffey	
2 Dec					Attilio Teruzzi		
1927 20 Nov		Pierre Bordes					
1928 18 Dec				Marshal Pietro Badoglio	Marshal Pietro Badoglio		
1929 Jan	Lucien Saint		François Manceron				
1930 3 Oct		Jules Carde					
1933 29 July			Marcel Peyrouton				

BRITISH/FRENCH/ITALIAN REPRESENTATIVES

REP (B)

	MOROCCO	ALGERIA	TUNISIA	LIBYA	SUDAN	SOUTHERN ARABIA
	Saint	Carde	Peyrouton	Badoglio	Maffey	
1933 Aug	Henri Ponsot					
6 Nov				Marshal Italo Balbo		
1934 10 Jan					Colonel Sir Stewart Symes	
1935 21 Sept		Georges Le Beau				
1936 22 Mar	Marcel Peyrouton					
17 Apr			Armand Guillon			
16 Sept	General Hippolite Noguès					
1937 1 Apr						Colonel Sir Bernard Reilly *(Note 79)*
1938 24 Oct			Eirik Labonne			
1940 1 July				Marshal Rodolfo Graziani *(Note 80)*		
20 July		Admiral Charles Abrial				
22 July			Admiral Jean-Pierre Esteva			
15 Oct					General Sir Hubert Huddleston	
24 Oct						Sir John Hathorn Hall
1941 20 Nov		Yves Chatel				
1943 19 Mar		Marcel Peyrouton				
10 May			General Charles Mast			

BRITISH/FRENCH/ITALIAN REPRESENTATIVES

REP (B)   **BRITISH/FRENCH/ITALIAN REPRESENTATIVES**

	MOROCCO	ALGERIA	TUNISIA	SUDAN	SOUTHERN ARABIA
	Noguès	Peyrouton	Mast	Huddleston	Hall
1943 3 June		General Georges Catroux			
5 June	Gabriel Puaux				
1944 Sept		Yves Chataigneau			
15 Dec					Sir Reginald Champion
1946 4 Mar	Eirik Labonne				
1947 22 Feb			Jean Mons		
8 Apr				Sir Robert Howe	
28 May	General Alphonse Juin				
1948 11 Feb		Marcel Naegelen			
1950 31 May			Louis Perillier		
1951 11 Apr		Roger Léonard			
Apr					Sir Tom Hickinbotham
28 Aug	General Augustin Guillaume				
24 Dec			Jean de Hautecloque		
1952 2 Sept			Pierre Voizard		
1954 20 May	Francis Lacoste				
31 July			General Pierre Boyer de Latour du Moulin		
1955 26 Jan		Jacques Soustelle			
11 Mar				Sir Knox Helm	
20 June	Gilbert Grandval				
29 Aug	General Pierre Boyer de Latour du Moulin				
13 Sept			Roger Seydoux		
9 Nov	André Dubois				
1956 1 Jan				*Independent*	
30 Jan		General Georges Catroux			

108

	MOROCCO	ALGERIA	TUNISIA	SUDAN	SOUTHERN ARABIA
	Dubois	Catroux	Seydoux	*Independent*	Hickinbotham
1956 10 Feb		Robert Lacoste			
2 Mar	*Independent*				
20 Mar			*Independent*		
13 July					Sir William Luce
1958 12 May		André Mutter			
1 June		General Raoul Salan			
12 Dec		Paul Delouvrier			
1960 23 Oct					Sir Charles Johnston
23 Nov		Jean Morin			
1962 19 Mar		Christian Fouchet			
3 July		*Independent*			
1963 5 June					Sir Kennedy Trevaskis
1964 21 Dec					Sir Richard Turnbull
1967 11 Mar					Sir Humphrey Trevelyan
30 Nov					*Independent*

BRITISH/FRENCH/ITALIAN FOREIGN AND COLONIAL MINISTERS   FOR/COL

	UNITED KINGDOM		FRANCE		ITALY	
	FOREIGN MINISTER	COLONIAL MINISTER	FOREIGN MINISTER	COLONIAL MINISTER	FOREIGN MINISTER	COLONIAL MINISTER
1900 1 Jan	Lord Salisbury	Joseph Chamberlain	Théophile Delcassé	Albert Decrais	Marchese Viscosti Venosta	*None*
1 Nov	Lord Landsdowne					
1901 14 Feb					Giulio Prinetti	
1902 8 June				Gaston Doumergue		
1903 9 Feb					Admiral Enrico Morin	
9 Oct		Alfred Lyttelton				
2 Nov					Tommaso Tittoni	
1905 24 Jan				Etienne Clémentel		
6 June			Maurice Rouvier			
11 Dec	Sir Edward Grey	Lord Elgin				
24 Dec					Marchese di San Giuliano	
1906 8 Feb					Count Francesco Guiccardini	
12 Mar			Léon Bourgeois	Georges Leygues		
28 May					Tommaso Tittoni	
23 Oct			Stephen Pichon	Raphael Milliès-Lacroix		
1908 16 Apr		Lord Crewe				
1909 24 July				Georges Trouillot		
10 Dec					Count Francesco Guiccardini	
1910 31 Mar					Marchese di San Giuliano	
3 Nov				Jean Morel		
7 Nov		Lewis Harcourt				
1911 27 Feb			Jean Cruppi	Adolphe Messimy		
27 June				Albert Lebrun		
28 June			Justin de Selves			
1912 13 Jan			Raymond Poincaré			

FOR/COL

	UNITED KINGDOM		FRANCE		ITALY	
	FOREIGN MINISTER	COLONIAL MINISTER	FOREIGN MINISTER	COLONIAL MINISTER	FOREIGN MINISTER	COLONIAL MINISTER
	Grey	Harcourt	Poincaré	Lebrun	San Giuliano	*None*
1912 21 Nov						Pietro Bertolini
1913 13 Jan				René Besnard		
21 Jan			Célestin Jonnart	Jean Morel		
21 Mar			Stephen Pichon			
8 Dec			Gaston Doumergue	Albert Lebrun		
1914 17 Mar						Ferdinando Martini
9 June			Léon Bourgeois	Maurice Maunoury		
13 June			René Viviani	Maurice Raynaud		
3 Aug			Gaston Doumergue			
26 Aug			Théophile Delcassé	Gaston Doumergue		
16 Oct					Antonio* Salandra	
5 Nov					Baron Sidney Sonnino	
1915 27 May		Andrew Bonar Law				
29 Oct			Aristide Briand			
1916 18 June						Gaspare Colosimo
11 Dec	Arthur James Balfour	Walter Long				
1917 20 Mar			Alexandre Ribot	André Maginot		
13 Sept				René Besnard		
23 Oct			Louis Barthou			
17 Nov			Stephen Pichon	Henry Simon		
1919 9 Jan		Lord Milner				
23 June					Tommaso Tittoni	
28 June						Luigi Rossi
24 Oct	Lord Curzon					
25 Nov					Vittorio Scialoja	

	UNITED KINGDOM		FRANCE		ITALY	
	FOREIGN MINISTER	COLONIAL MINISTER	FOREIGN MINISTER	COLONIAL MINISTER	FOREIGN MINISTER	COLONIAL MINISTER
	Curzon	Milner	Pichon	Simon	Scialoja	Rossi
1920 20 Jan			Alexandre Millerand	Albert Sarraut		
20 Mar						Francesco Nitti
21 May						Meuccio Ruini
15 June					Count Carlo Sforza	Luigi Rossi
24 Sept			Georges Leygues			
1921 16 Jan			Aristide Briand			
14 Feb		Winston Spencer Churchill				
4 July					Marchese della Torretta	Giuseppe Girardini
1922 15 Jan			Raymond Poincaré			
25 Feb					Dr Carlo Schanzer	Professor Giovanni Amendola
25 Oct		Duke of Devonshire				
30 Oct					Benito Mussolini	Luigi Federzoni
1924 23 Jan	James Ramsay MacDonald	James Henry Thomas				

FOR/COL

FOR/COL

		UNITED KINGDOM		FRANCE		ITALY	
		FOREIGN MINISTER	COLONIAL MINISTER OF	FOREIGN MINISTER	COLONIAL MINISTER	FOREIGN MINISTER	COLONIAL MINISTER
			Colonies / Dominions				
1924	28 Mar	MacDonald	Thomas	Poincaré	Sarraut / Jean Fabry	Mussolini	Federzoni
	8 June			Edmond Lefebvre du Prey			
	15 June			Edouard Herriot	Edouard Daladier		
	30 June						Prince Pietro Lanza di Scalèa
	7 Nov	Sir Austen Chamberlain	Leopold Amery / Leopold Amery				
1925	17 Apr			Aristide Briand	André Hesse		
	29 Oct				Léon Perrier		
1926	20 July			Edouard Herriot	Adrien Darriac		
	23 July			Aristide Briand	Léon Perrier		
	5 Nov						Luigi Federzoni
1928	11 Nov				André Maginot		
	18 Dec						Benito Mussolini
1929	8 June	Arthur Henderson	Sidney Webb Lord Passfield / Sidney Webb Lord Passfield				
	12 Sept					Count Dino Grandi	General Emilio de Bono
	2 Nov				François Piétri		
1930	21 Feb				Lucien Lamoureux		
	2 Mar				François Piétri		
	13 June		James Henry Thomas				
	13 Dec				Théodore Steeg		
1931	27 Jan				Paul Reynaud		
	26 Aug	Lord Reading	James Henry Thomas				
	9 Nov	Sir John Simon	Sir Philip Cunliffe-Lister Lord Swinton				
1932	14 Jan			Pierre Laval			

114

FOR/COL

	UNITED KINGDOM			FRANCE		ITALY	
	FOREIGN MINISTER	COLONIAL MINISTER OF Colonies	Dominions	FOREIGN MINISTER	COLONIAL MINISTER	FOREIGN MINISTER	COLONIAL MINISTER
	Simon	Lister	Thomas	Laval	Reynaud	Grandi	de Bono
1932 20 Feb				André Tardieu	Louis de Chappedelaine		
3 June				Edouard Herriot			
8 June					Albert Sarraut		
20 July						Benito Mussolini	
18 Dec				Joseph Paul-Boncour			
1933 26 Oct					François Piétri		
26 Nov					Albert Dalimier		
1934 9 Jan					Lucien Lamoureux		
30 Jan				Edouard Daladier	Henry de Jouvenel		
9 Feb				Louis Barthou	Pierre Laval		
9 Oct				Pierre Laval			
13 Oct					Louis Rollin		
1935 16 Jan							Benito Mussolini
7 June	Sir Samuel Hoare	Malcolm MacDonald					
27 Nov		James Henry Thomas	Malcolm MacDonald				
23 Dec	Anthony Eden						
1936 24 Jan				Pierre-Etienne Flandin	Jacques Stern		
29 May		William Ormsby Gore Lord Harlech					
4 June				Yvon Delbos	Marius Moutet		
9 June						Count Galeazzo Ciano	Allessandro Lessona
1937 20 Nov							Benito Mussolini
1938 18 Jan					Théodore Steeg		
22 Feb	Lord Halifax						

115

FOR/COL

	UNITED KINGDOM			FRANCE		ITALY	
	FOREIGN MINISTER	COLONIAL MINISTER OF Colonies	Dominions	FOREIGN MINISTER	COLONIAL MINISTER	FOREIGN MINISTER	COLONIAL MINISTER
	Halifax	Gore	MacDonald	Delbos	Steeg	Ciano	Mussolini
1938 13 Mar				Joseph Paul-Boncour	Marius Moutet		
10 Apr				Georges Bonnet	Georges Mandel		
16 May		Malcolm MacDonald	Lord Stanley				
4 Nov			Malcolm MacDonald				
1939 2 Feb			Sir Thomas Inskip Lord Caldecote				
4 Sept			Anthony Eden				
15 Sept				Edouard Daladier			
31 Oct							Ottilio Terruzzi
1940 21 Mar				Paul Reynaud			
15 May		Lord Lloyd	Lord Caldecote				
18 May				Edouard Daladier	Louis Rollin		
6 June				Paul Reynaud			
17 June				Paul Baudouin	Albert Rivière		
6 Sept					Admiral Platon		
4 Oct			Lord Cranborne				
28 Oct				Pierre Laval			
15 Dec				Pierre-Etienne Flandin			
23 Dec	Anthony Eden						
1941 8 Feb		Lord Moyne					
9 Feb				Admiral François Darlan			
1942 18 Feb		Lord Cranborne	Clement Attlee				
18 Apr				Pierre Laval	Brévié		
22 Nov		Oliver Stanley					
1943 5 Feb						Benito Mussolini	

FOR/COL

	UNITED KINGDOM			FRANCE		ITALY	
	FOREIGN MINISTER	COLONIAL MINISTER OF Colonies	Dominions	FOREIGN MINISTER	COLONIAL MINISTER	FOREIGN MINISTER	COLONIAL MINISTER
	Eden	Stanley	Attlee	Laval	Brévié	Mussolini	Terruzzi
1943 28 Mar					Admiral Bléhaut		
26 July						Baron Raffaele Guariglia	Melchiade de Gabba (last holder of post)
24 Sept			Lord Cranborne				
9 Nov				René Massigli	René Pleven		
1944 21 Apr						Marshal Pietro Badoglio	
9 June						Ivanoe Bonomi	
10 Sept				Georges Bidault			
15 Nov					Paul Giacobi		
10 Dec						Alcide de Gasperi	
1945 26 July	Ernest Bevin	George Henry Hall	Lord Addison				
17 Oct						Pietro Nenni	
21 Nov					Jacques Soustelle		
1946 27 Jan					Marius Moutet		
16 Dec				Léon Blum			
1947 22 Jan				Georges Bidault			
2 Feb						Count Carlo Sforza	
7 Oct		Arthur Creech Jones	Philip Noel-Baker				
23 Oct					Paul Ramadier		
24 Nov					Paul Coste-Floret		
1948 26 July				Robert Schuman			
1949 28 Oct					Paul Letourneau		

FOR/COL

		UNITED KINGDOM			FRANCE		ITALY	
		FOREIGN MINISTER	COLONIAL MINISTER OF Colonies	Commonwealth Relations	FOREIGN MINISTER	COLONIAL MINISTER	FOREIGN MINISTER	COLONIAL MINISTER
		Bevin	Jones	Baker	Schuman	Letourneau	Sforza	
1950	28 Feb		James Griffiths	Patrick Gordon Walker				
	2 July					Paul Coste-Floret		
	12 July					François Mitterand		
1951	9 Mar	Herbert Morrison						
	26 July						Alcide de Gasperi	
	11 Aug					Louis Jacquinot		
	26 Oct		Oliver Lyttleton	General Lord Ismay				
	27 Oct	Anthony Eden						
1952	8 Mar				Pierre Pfimlin			
	12 Mar			Lord Salisbury				
	24 Nov			Lord Swinton				
1953	8 Jan				Georges Bidault	Louis Jacquinot		
	19 June					Robert Buron		
	28 July		Alan Lennox-Boyd					
	17 Aug						Giuseppe Pella	
1954	18 Jan						Attilio Piccioni	
	19 June				Pierre Mendès-France			
	18 Sept						Gaetano Martino	
1955	20 Jan				Edgar Faure	Jean-Jacques Juglas		
	23 Feb				Antoine Pinay	Pierre-Henri Tietgen		
	6 Apr	Harold Macmillan						
	12 Apr			Lord Home				
	20 Dec	Selwyn Lloyd						

FOR/COL

	UNITED KINGDOM			FRANCE		ITALY	
	FOREIGN MINISTER	COLONIAL MINISTER OF Colonies	Commonwealth Relations	FOREIGN MINISTER	COLONIAL MINISTER	FOREIGN MINISTER	COLONIAL MINISTER
	Lloyd	Lennox-Boyd	Home	Pinay	Tietgen	Martino	
1956 31 Jan				Christian Pineau	Gaston Deferre		
1957 20 May						Giuseppe Pella	
11 June					Gérard Jacquet		
1958 12 May				René Pleven	André Colin		
2 June				Maurice Couve de Murville	Bernard Cornut-Gentille		
1 July						Amintore Fanfani	
1959 8 Jan					Robert Lecourt		
16 Feb						Giuseppe Pella	
14 Oct		Iain Macleod					
1960 8 Feb					Roger Frey		
25 Mar						Antonio Segni	
27 July	Lord Home		Duncan Sandys				
1961 18 May					*Posts divided*		
24 Aug					Louis Jacquinot		
9 Oct		Reginald Maudling					
1962 29 May						Attilio Piccioni	
16 July		Duncan Sandys					
1963 20 Oct	Richard Austen Butler						
4 Dec						Giuseppe Saragat	
1964 16 Oct	Patrick Gordon Walker	Anthony Greenwood	Arthur Bottomley				
29 Dec						Aldo Moro	
1965 22 Jan	Michael Stewart						
5 Mar						Amintore Fanfani	
22 Dec		Lord Longford					

FOR/COL

	UNITED KINGDOM			FRANCE		ITALY	
		COLONIAL MINISTER OF					
	FOREIGN MINISTER	Colonies	Commonwealth Relations	FOREIGN MINISTER	COLONIAL MINISTER	FOREIGN MINISTER	COLONIAL MINISTER
	Stewart	Longford	Bottomley	Couve de Murville	Jacquinot	Fanfani	
1966 9 Jan					General Pierre Billotte		
5 Apr		Fred Lee					
31 July		*Merged with CRO*					
10 Aug	George Brown		Herbert Bowden				
1967 28 Aug			George Thomson				
1968 15 Mar	Michael Stewart						
31 May				Michel Debré	Joel Le Theule		
24 June						Giuseppe Medici	
11 July					Michel Inchauspé		
17 Oct			*Merged with Foreign Office*				
12 Dec						Pietro Nenni	
1969 22 June				Maurice Schumann	Henri Rey		
5 Aug						Aldo Moro	
1970 19 June	Sir Alec Douglas-Home						
1971 25 Feb					Pierre Messmer		
1972 26 June						Giuseppe Medici	
6 July					Xavier Deniau		

Notes

1. The French occupation of Damascus on this date put an end to the independent Syrian monarchy.
2. The French reimposed direct rule.
3. A provisional Government to supervise elections.
4. This is the date of the formal appointment of Abd al-Nasir as President of the United Arab Republic.
5. There was no Head of State after the Revolution but a Council of Sovereignty which originally consisted of General Najib al-Rubai, Muhammad Mahdi Kubbah and Khalid al-Naqshabandi.
6. When Syria broke away from the United Arab Republic there was no immediate proclamation of a new Head of State.
7. General Atasi, after seizing power in a coup, took the title of President of the Revolutionary Command Council.
8. Mulai Hafid revolted against his brother some months earlier and was proclaimed Sultan in different cities on different dates. The date given is that of his recognition by the *ulama* of Fez.
9. Mulai ben Arafa was put in power by the French after they had exiled the legitimate Sultan, Sidi Muhammad ben Yussef. Sidi Muhammad returned to his country on 17 November 1955.
10. General Abboud, after seizing power in a coup, took the title of President of the Supreme Council.
11. General Nimeiri, after seizing power in a coup, took the title of President of the Revolutionary Council.
12. Shaykh Isa, who had been installed by the British in 1869, was forced by the Imperial authorities to hand over effective power to his son and eventual successor Shaykh Hamad in 1923.
13. Shaykh Jasim was the effective Ruler of Qatar from the 1870s until his death, although his brother Ahmad was the nominal Shaykh until he was murdered in December 1905.
14. I have somewhat arbitrarily dated ibn Saud's reign from his recapture of Riyadh. He did not control the whole of Arabia until after his conquest of the Hejaz in 1925-6. The name 'Saudi Arabia' was adopted in 1932.
15. Fujayrah was officially regarded as being under the suzerainty of Sharjah until 1952.
16. This was the date of the official recognition of the independence of Fujayrah although Shaykh Muhammad had been its effective ruler since the 1930s.
17. Owing to the extreme old age of his father, Shaykh Rashid had been the effective Ruler since the 1940s.
18. This was the first formal Cabinet. Before that there had been a Council of Directors.
19. This was originally a Provisional Government but subsequently was formally constituted after the establishment of the Monarchy.
20. His official title was President of the Federal Council of Syria.
21. Ministers were abolished and Directors were appointed for the various Departments.
22. Ministers were abolished and executive powers put in the hands of Abdallah Bayhum as Secretary of State.
23. This Ministry was overthrown by a coup without actually taking office.
24. Although al-Yafi was formally appointed Prime Minister he did not succeed in forming a Government.
25. It is not clear if al-Nimr succeeded in forming a Government. *The Summary of World*

Broadcasts says that no list of Ministers was given over Amman Radio although a list was announced by Damascus.

26. Syria was formally absorbed into the United Arab Republic and a joint Ministry formed.

27. The Arab Federation (a union of Iraq and Jordan) was formed with some joint Ministers while each country also retained its own Ministers. General Nuri Pasha al-Said was named Prime Minister of the Federation.

28. His official title was President of the Executive Council.

29. There were Prime Ministers throughout the period of the French Protectorate but they had little effective power.

30. This was a Government in exile but was recognised by many countries.

31. This was the first formally constituted Cabinet in Saudi Arabia. Before that Ministers had been individually responsible to the King.

32. This was the first formally constituted Cabinet in the Yemen. There had previously been Ministers, including a Premier, Sayf al-Islam al-Hassan ben Yahya, who were individually responsible to the Imam.

33. With the proclamation of a British Protectorate over Egypt, the post of Minister of Foreign Affairs was abolished.

34. Tawfiq al-Suwaydi was appointed Minister of Foreign Affairs for the Federation of Iraq and Jordan.

35. Dr Fawzi was appointed Deputy Prime Minister for Foreign Affairs and Dr Riad Minister of Foreign Affairs.

36. Dr Riad was appointed Deputy Prime Minister and Foreign Minister and Dr Ghaleb Minister of State for Foreign Affairs.

37. Prince Faysal had been Minister of Foreign Affairs for many years before the constitution of the first formal Cabinet. Among his predecessors in the 1930s was Dr Abdallah al-Damluji, who was later Minister of Foreign Affairs in Iraq. As Prince Faysal was also Prime Minister from 1954 much of the detailed work was done by Shaykh Yusuf Yasin.

38. The Crown Prince was Minister of Foreign Affairs in the first formally constituted Cabinet. During the reign of the Imam Yahya the Qadi, Muhammad Raghib was in charge of external relations which were later in the hands of Prince Abdallah ben Yahya. While the Crown Prince remained nominally in charge of the Ministry until his accession to the throne, day-to-day affairs were usually dealt with by Abd al-Rahman Abu Talib before 1961 and after that date by Hassan Ibrahim.

39. Although Faysal has continued to be Minister of Foreign Affairs until the present day, much of the detailed work has been done recently by Umar al-Saqqaf.

40. The names given are those of the Deputy Premiers for Foreign Affairs. The actual portfolio was held by Ahmad Qaid Barakat.

41. Mulqi seems to have been appointed some months before his name appears in a Cabinet list of this day. I have, however, been unable to find an exact date.

42. Sulayman Tuqan, the Jordanian Defence Minister, also held the post in the central Government of the Arab Federation.

43. Some sources state that from 2 July 1960 to 21 December 1960 Prince Musa'id ben Abd al-Rahman was Minister of Defence. However, I have accepted that Prince Fahad continued in office until he was relieved by Royal Decree No. 35 of 21 December 1960.

44. General Amri held the appointment of Commander in Chief rather than that of Minister of War. On his resignation in July 1969, the office of Commander in Chief was divided amongst several Deputies. No Minister of War, by this title, has appeared in any subsequent Cabinet list. However in the Cabinet of 2 September 1969 Ali Saif al-Kholani was appointed Deputy Premier for Military Affairs (as well as Security and Youth). Amri resumed the post of Commander in Chief and held it until his exile in 1971, when the rank was abolished.

45. Colonel Oldman has the title of Secretary (not Minister) of Defence.

46. When the United Arab Republic was formed, two Ministers of the Interior, Mohieddin and al-Sarraj, were nominated. In practice the former was in charge of the Southern Region (Egypt) while the other administered the Northern (Syria).

47. When the new form of unified Government was created, al-Sarraj was named Vice-President in charge of the Interior for both Regions while Radwan was Minister of the Interior for both Regions.

48. Abd al-Salam Sabra was Deputy Prime Minister for Internal Affairs. The Minister of the Interior was Colonel Muhammad Abd al-Wali. In al-Qirshimi's Cabinet of September 1969 Abd al-Salam Sabra continued as Deputy Prime Minister while Colonel Muhammad Margham was Minister for Internal Affairs.

49. Shaykh Badr was Minister of the Interior in the first formally constituted Omani Cabinet. Under Sultan Said the post was held for many years by Shaykh Abdallah ben Ibrahim.

50. Abd al-Salam Sabra was appointed Deputy Prime Minister for Internal Affairs. The Minister of the Interior was Abdallah Husayn Barakat.

51. Colonel al-Hamidi was appointed Deputy Prime Minister for Internal Affairs. The Minister of the Interior was Brigadier Sallal al-Razihi. He was followed by Colonel Ali Saif al-Kholani on 16 April 1972.

52. On 18 May 1958 Abd al-Karim al-Uzri became Finance Minister of the new Iraq-Jordanian Federation. Dr Nadim al-Pachachi was appointed Finance Minister for Iraq while Anastas Hananiyah continued in Jordan.

53. The Egyptian al-Qaysuni became Minister of the Economy for the United Arab Republic, assisted by Khalil Kallas for the Syrian Region.

54. Shuqayr was appointed Minister of Economy and Planning while al-Qaysuni was Deputy Premier in charge of Economic Affairs.

55. The date given is that of the first formally constituted Cabinet of Saudi Arabia. Shaykh Abdallah Sulayman had in fact been Minister of Finance since 1929.

56. The date given is that of the first formally constituted Cabinet in the Yemen. I have found no reference to a Minister of Finance in any book before this date.

57. As Crown Prince Faysal held numerous other posts, Shaykh Abdallah ben Adwan was usually in charge of the Ministry of Finance as Minister of State.

58. Abd al-Ghani Ali Ahmad was Minister of the Treasury. At various times there were Deputy Premiers for Economic and Treasury Affairs (Muhammad Ali Uthman in October 1963 and Colonel Abdallah Jizaylan in May 1964), as well as Minister of the Economy (Ali Saif al-Kholani in May 1964).

59. Ahmad Abduh was Minister of the Treasury. Muhammad Said Attar was Minister of the Economy.

60. Colonel Ahmad al-Rahumi was Minister of the Treasury while Muhammad Ali Uthman was Deputy Premier for Financial and Economic Affairs and Muhsin al-Sirri Minister of the Economy.

61. Shaykh Sabah and his successor were also Ministers of Oil.

62. On 12 October 1967 Dr Muhammad Said Attar was made Minister of the Economy while Abd al-Ghani Ali Ahmad continued Minister of the Treasury.

63. Dr Muhammad Said Attar continued as Minister of the Economy.

64. Colonel Ahmad al-Rahumi was Minister of the Treasury and Abd al-Aziz Abd al-Ghani was Minister of the Economy.

65. This Cabinet had also a Deputy Premier for Foreign and Economic Affairs, Husayn Ali al-Hubayshi, a Minister for the Economy, Muhammad Anam Ghalib and a President's Adviser for Economic Affairs, Ahmad Abduh Said.

66. This Cabinet had a Deputy Premier for Financial Affairs, Ahmad Abduh Said while Muhammad Anam Ghalib continued Minister of the Economy.

67. This Cabinet also had a Deputy Premier for the Economy, Dr Muhammad Said Attar, and a Deputy Premier for Finance, Ahmad Abduh Said. On 7 June Yahya Jughman was appointed Deputy Premier for Economic Affairs.

68. Shaykh Khalifa was also Minister for Oil.

69. This Cabinet also had a Minister for the Economy, Ahmad Abduh Said.

70. Abdallah al-Shibani was Minister for Finance while Dr Muhammad Said Attar was Deputy Premier for Financial Affairs and Minister of the Economy.

71. On 8 July 1972 Hassan Makki was appointed Deputy Premier for Economic Affairs.

72. The British Representative in Egypt had the title of British Agent and Consul-General until the proclamation of the Protectorate in December 1914. He was then called the High Commissioner until December 1936, when he became an Ambassador.

73. The French Representative in the Levant had the title of Haut-Commissaire.

74. The first title of the British Representative in Iraq (then Mesopotamia) was Chief Political Officer. Cox later became Civil Commissioner. Wilson was appointed Acting Civil Commissioner. Cox returned in 1920 as High Commissioner and this title continued until 1932, when Humphrys' title was changed to Ambassador.

75. The High Commissioner for Palestine was responsible for British relations with Trans-Jordan and the names given are those of the High Commissioners. The resident British representatives in the country were 1921-4 H. St J. B. Philby, 1924-39 Colonel (Sir) Henry Cox and 1939-52 Sir Alec Kirkbride.

76. As Morocco was a Protectorate, the French Representative had the title of Résident Général.

77. Until 1956 the French Representative in Algeria had the title of Gouverneur Général. Lacoste was Minister for Algeria. Salan and Delouvrier were entitled Délégué Général. Fouchet was Haut Commissaire.

78. French Representatives in Tunisia were called Résident Général except for the last who was Haut-Commissaire.

79. The British Representative in Aden was styled Resident until 1937, when he became Governor. Reilly had in fact been there since 1931.

80. British forces overran Libya 1942/3 and the Italian administration came to an end.